THE SECRET FOOTBALLER'S GUIDE TO THE MODERN GAME

THE SECRET FOOTBALLER'S GUIDE TO THE MODERN GAME

Tips and Tactics from the Ultimate Insider

First published in 2014
by Guardian Books, Kings Place, 90 York Way, London N1 9GU
and Faber and Faber Ltd, Bloomsbury House, 74–77 Great Russell
Street, London WC1B 3DA

This edition first published 2014

2 4 6 8 10 9 7 5 3 1

A CIP catalogue record for this book is available
from the British Library

ISBN 978-1783-35062-9

Text design by carrdesignstudio.com
Illustrations by Pete Guest
Printed and bound by CPI Group (UK) Ltd, Croydon, CR0 4YY

*Publisher's note: Some identifying features have been altered in this
book to protect the Secret Footballer's identity.*

For my mother and father and my wife and children. Yes, my parents drove me to games as a kid and yes, my family have put up with a lot from me over the seasons … but they've all gone on an incredible journey too and that's always worth pointing out.

CONTENTS

CONTENTS

'Of the 95 per cent of people who love football,
only 2 per cent understand it. One of my best friends
is a complete fan, sees everything, knows everything.
But he has no idea . . . It's complicated.'

Xavi

INTRODUCTION

Whatever you think of that quote from Barcelona's legendary playmaker, Xavi Hernández, he's right. Only 2 per cent of people truly understand football, and the vast majority of those 2 per cent of people are involved in the game, week in and week out. They are the players and managers who are paid to win football matches, who understand what it takes to win football matches and who know how to change the course of a football match with a single decision – while retaining the courage of their convictions to make that decision, even when those around them are scratching their heads in wonderment.

While it is true that some things in this game will forever remain the privilege of the people who are involved day to day, that doesn't necessarily mean that the fans paying their money to sit in the stands aren't allowed an opinion or can never be educated, at least from a tactical standpoint. Unfortunately, many people on the outside looking in are at the mercy of the 'wisdom' of others who also have no direct involvement in football.

Books on football tactics, strategies and formations need an angle because, ultimately, the authors need to sell books, and I suppose it says everything when a team of economists who have never kicked a ball in their lives can persuade football fans to buy books on the game. Such books may have taken subject matter that looks great as a series of numbers on a page but which, in reality, has no relationship with the way that Solskjaer instinctively knew where to stand from Beckham's corner in the last minute of the 1999 Champions League final, or how Lionel Messi dribbles the ball by looking at the feet of his opponents, or what it means to stand in front of your home fans while holding a trophy above your head. A person can have as many letters after his name as he likes but only the players really know what this game feels like; we are the only ones who can try to describe what it feels like to score against Manchester United or beat Arsenal or win a trophy.

Most of the books that try to explain what really happens in modern football have the sole aim of bombarding you with statistics to labour a point that doesn't and never will exist. But I get it – they're fun because they deal with historical data that evokes a sense of nostalgia in the reader. I have read books that claim teams should sell their best players; I have read books that claim the influx of foreign players in the Premier League is benefiting the England team; and I have read books that claim the manager isn't important.

This book tells you how football actually works in the real world. It isn't written by a journalist, it isn't written by a couple of Harvard economists – it's written by a footballer who can tell you exactly why things work the way they work, having experienced them first-hand. *The Guide to the Modern Game* is written by me, the Secret Footballer.

GETTING STARTED

Fitness

When I became a professional footballer I thought that the standard of the players would leave me with a lot to learn in a short space of time. I was wrong. However, the fitness training in pre-season was unlike anything that I had experienced before – but although I took everything that was flung at me, I later learned that my new manager, my first as a professional, had a reputation for going overboard when it came to getting his squad fit. I now know that he was slightly mad and a little ahead of the curve in terms of the latest theories on fitness and nutrition. He had studied what the top sides were doing in Italy to help their players and, as a result, had uncovered tales of incredible recovery aids such as creatine, a supplementary white powder that helps tired muscles recover twice as fast as conventional methods. He had new pills that helped lubricate the joints to avoid stiffness, and he had reams of paper with specific training methods suited to whatever particular training that he wanted the players to do. Unfortunately, one of those training exercises was called 'fartlek'. We laughed when we first heard it, of course, but two days later, at the end of the first fartlek run, we couldn't get our breath and we certainly weren't laughing.

Fartlek training, or 'the fartlek run', is still in use today, and is particularly prevalent with teams lower down the divisions that don't have access to £10,000 training vests or the equipment to carry out more individual testing that is football based. In fact, fartlek has been around for many years in one form or another; it was originally developed by a Swedish coach called Gösta Holmér in 1937. The Swedish cross-country team had lost regularly to their Finnish counterparts in the 1920s – something that had caused great embarrassment to the Swedes – and so Holmér developed a continuous and interval training technique that would work a person both aerobically (low intensity, between 60 per cent and 85 per cent of the maximum heart rate) and anaerobically (high intensity, at maximum effort for a few seconds or up to two minutes).

I hated it. The run was always an hour long, and consisted of running full-on for 30 seconds, then jogging for a minute. Much like the drinking game so beloved of players, where you have a shot of beer every minute for an hour, it sounds easy. By the end you are left hanging on for dear life and, in those final moments of the run, you wish that you'd forfeited those last twenty minutes in Vegas, where drinking another shot of Budweiser felt like drinking petrol.

Lots of footballers do the fartlek run on their own throughout June, before they have to go back to their clubs to start pre-season proper on 1 July. If, in the evening, you see a guy in a hoodie running between lampposts, jogging between two and sprinting between the next two, it's not some kind of bizarre getaway with a nod towards keeping fit, it's a footballer being busy.

The latest research all points towards 'sport specific' fitness work. That is to say: if you play football for a living then you should get fit by playing football. That doesn't mean playing eleven-a-side football every day; it means doing some pretty tough fitness work, but using the ball in a way that you would in a game. There has been much bastardising of this information among fitness coaches, though – after all, when and why do I need to dribble the ball between a set of cones, around a pole and back to the start? I may be using a ball but the drill is certainly not specific to my game.

FIVE SPECIFIC FOOTBALL DRILLS TO GET FIT IN PRE-SEASON

⊙ Two against two, with one goalkeeper in a full-sized goal, playing only in the penalty area. This is a 'one-on, one-off' drill, which means that the first four individuals play for three minutes, before resting for three minutes, while the next four individuals play. The session can be made harder by reducing the number of touches each player is allowed. Believe me, after three minutes of three touches you'll need an oxygen tent. Great for two strikers to go together against two defenders.

⊙ Take a five-a-side pitch and split it into thirds. Take three teams of six players and put a team at either end, with a 'working team' in the middle third. Two players from the working team chase the ball into one of the end thirds, trying to win it back from a team of six who have to get to ten passes using one touch each before they transfer the ball to the other end; the four remaining players in the middle are allowed to cut out the transferred pass. The two chasing the ball keep going to either end until they win it back and change with one of the other teams once all six players have had a go. The team with the most transfers against it loses. Perfect for midfielders closing players down.

⊙ Three teams of eight, with different coloured bibs on a half-sized pitch. Two teams always keep the ball while the other team tries to win it back. When the team chasing the ball finally win the ball back they keep it away from the team that gave the ball away together with the third team. There is always one team that gets a good run around, and the secret is to spread out around the square and have two people in the middle to provide wall passes. This session works on fitness through closing down and winning the ball back and also focuses on picking the right moment to switch the ball once the team chasing has squeezed right in.

⊙ Two teams play against each other on any size pitch while one team has to score in any goal and the other team just has to keep the ball. It is surprisingly easy to keep the ball without scoring, and very difficult for the other team to actually score. This drill really highlights the belief that the team keeping the ball conserves more energy than the team trying to win it back, because when the team trying to score actually win the ball back they are nearly always too tired to counterattack and try to score – in fact, they are nearly always too tired to just keep the ball and get a breather. As a result, the other team nearly always wins the ball back within six passes. It is a great fitness drill but it is also a great drill to show a squad of players how important it is to keep the ball in professional football.

☻ The attackers and midfielders start spread out across the halfway line while the defence start to the sides of the goal. The goalkeeper takes a goal-kick that an attacker controls and sets off towards the goal with three of his teammates. The defence run on to the pitch and hold the line that they think is right. Generally, this is a session for defenders as four attackers will always come from the halfway line, but they will attack two defenders, then three and then four. The last in the series of these drills introduces a midfielder that chases the four attacking players back towards the goal on the sound of a whistle. As soon as the move breaks down the defenders and attackers swap turns with another set that are ready to go once another goal-kick is taken. It is amazing how quickly the jelly legs set in, especially for the defenders.

In short, lots of fitness coaches, even in the Premier League, do not subscribe to the proven theory that basing a pre-season only on playing football will get players fully fit. In Italy the players have been undergoing such training since the mid-1980s, and it stands to reason that if you can get a squad of players fit while at the same time becoming more and more accustomed to manipulating the ball at high speed before the season has even started, then the likelihood is that you will have a much better chance of going into the opening day of the campaign at full throttle. The first manager I heard of who introduced a ball into every element of pre-season training was José Mourinho, and I was even told that he'd introduced a club policy whereby it became a fine for any player caught touching the ball with his hands during training.

So why doesn't every manager go for ball-specific pre-season training? After all, if it's good enough for José it ought to be good enough for everybody, right? Well, the truth is, most managers just don't trust the players to give their all in each training session, and there are reasons for that.

At Chelsea, and most other Premier League clubs, the players now wear £10,000 GPS vests (standing for Global Positioning System) over their kit. The vests track heart rate, distance covered, intensity and direction (amongst other things) during each training session, all of which means that fitness coaches can now tell exactly what sort of effort a player is putting in. Anybody 'tossing it off' is pulled up and reprimanded, but that is rare – at the top level you won't find too many individuals who are found wanting in training or matches. The rest of the non-elite sides tend to have to rely on the old-fashioned method of running their players round and round the pitch until they are either dying or dead.

But, budgets aside, don't forget that we are still playing in an era where, in order to get fit in pre-season, our managers ran up and down the stairs of the main stand – and the mantra seems to be that if it was good enough for them, then it's certainly good enough for us. I'm afraid that where a lot of managers and pre-season training is concerned, progress comes about one funeral at a time.

The five worst pre-season runs I've ever had to do

⚽ In Austria we had two sessions before breakfast that almost broke me: swimming relays in a 5°C mountain lake at 6 a.m. (two African players nearly drowned and had to be fished out by three other players) followed by a weights and core session at 7.30 a.m. back at the hotel. And just when you're looking forward to a decent breakfast at 9 a.m., you remember that it consists of fresh grapefruit, brown toast and All-Bran. Never mind, at 11 a.m. the running starts. I hate pre-season.

⚽ Early on in my career I had a manager who used to love cycling along the river. Unfortunately, twenty of his squad, including me, were running after him. In 30°C heat we ran down the river on a beautiful summer's day. The problem with running down the river is that it's very easy to work out that every step forward is another step that has to be taken on the way back and, these days, we know that being able to see the end or knowing how far you have to run beforehand is a huge advantage psychologically which makes players try harder to finish the run faster. As we're running down the river, we suddenly hear a loud cheer coming from the other bank where a group of people – my friends – are lying on the grass, shirts off, drinking cider. That was a hard run, and coming back was even harder. Thank God we didn't have camera phones back then.

☺ Later in my career a well-regarded fitness coach went out for a run along the beach during a pre-season tour and came back to the hotel where we were staying with tales of huge sand dunes, 40 feet high, that would be perfect for an impromptu running session for the players. The result was a bus down to the beach followed by ten runs at full pace from the bottom of the sand dune to the top, and then back down again with a 30-second rest in between runs. It was made worse by the fact that I trod on a piece of broken glass on the ninth run and spewed up for the first time in my career shortly after the tenth. Fortunately, I wasn't the only one, and there was a particular sense of achievement after that run that I haven't come across too often in football. People often talk about team bonding and the fact that a night out or a trip to the races can be good for team relations – and they can – but twenty-five players embracing each other after they've pulled each other through a really hard running session is one of the most underrated ways to build bridges in a squad.

☺ At the very start of pre-season a fitness level needs to be determined by the fitness coaches. A recent addition to football, but not to sport, is the 1000-metre run designed by the Chinese Olympic coaching team, who worked out that the time taken for somebody to run that distance would give them an exact figure with which to tailor an entirely individualised training programme. Unfortunately for football players, the translation of this method has been misunderstood, bastardised or, in some cases, both. The upshot is that a couple of years ago we did the same session for a week that involved 8 x 1000-metre runs with a four-a-side game on a half-size pitch in between them. In those games every player had to cross the halfway line when his team had scored, and every player had to cross the halfway line if the opposition were about to score; if you hadn't managed to recover over the halfway line then the opposition goal counted as two. The first 1000-metre runs, roughly two-and-three-quarters of the way around a cricket field, saw times of 3 minutes 30 seconds. The last run saw the time jump to 4 minutes and 30 seconds.

⊗ Not exactly a run but in the middle of my career I met a very forward-thinking sports scientist who based all of his pre-season training on a type of high-intensity interval training called 'Tabata'. This training is named after the Chinese professor who invented it, Izumi Tabata, and was originally used to benefit Chinese Olympic speed skaters. It involves 20 seconds of maximum intensity cardiovascular activity, followed by 10 seconds of rest, repeated for eight cycles (4 minutes) at a VO_2 max of 170 per cent. At that particular club, Tabata training was used on the cycling machine, the rowing machine and as part of a superset weights programme; it is recognised internationally as one of, if not *the* fastest way to gain fitness when used at least four times a week.

THE VO_2 MAX TEST

Whatever training method a manager and his coaches decide to go with, the exact benefit is difficult, if not impossible, to gauge unless you have a barometer of a player's fitness levels from the start. In 1850 a German physician called Adolf Eugen Fick, a man who clearly hated people, came up with the first equations for measuring a person's cardiac output. Over time his findings would become more refined until, many years later, his initial discovery would come to be known in sports institutions around the world as the dreaded VO_2 max test.

The real benefit of a run like this lies in doing it again when a player comes back from the off-season. So the secret is to put in a fairly good time that reflects the fact that you have tried, while not being near your absolute maximum. Therefore when you come to do the test again, after your holidays and the booze and the shisha pipes and the shocking diet, you will be able to beat the original score, thus appearing to those who care about these statistics that you have been working hard in the off-season.

Now, that may sound deceitful, probably because it is, but as you get older you'll realise that people watch your scores very keenly, and the moment that a 34-, 35- or 36-year-old falls off the edge of the fitness levels required, he will be out the door to the lower levels. The job of a player is to do everything he possibly can to prolong that inevitability – if that's what he wants, of course.

Remember, you can't cheat the actual VO_2 itself – the software tells those monitoring the run exactly when the body can't take in enough oxygen to replace the energy it is expending. That generally happens around the 7-minute mark at a 1.0 incline and at a 15.5 pace setting. Thereafter, what is actually being tested is how long the body can continue to run simply by using its own reserves; that is the real test of how fit a player is. If you get to 11 or 12 minutes then you're doing pretty well – lots of players fall in at around 10 minutes 30 seconds. It is this part of the test that, ideally, you want to lop 30 seconds off. If you think you can get to 11 minutes then stop at 10 minutes 30 seconds.

When you come back from the off-season you'll have a much better chance of hitting 10 minutes 30 seconds again, and if you can better that mark then it will give the impression that you have been working hard in your time off. You should be working hard anyway, of course, but, for me, going to the gym every day simply isn't an option in the summer. It may sound ridiculous to say so, but I only have six weeks to meet and catch up with all the people that need my attention, and that makes regular training very easy to talk myself out of.

Today, the VO_2 max test is still torture, and has been made worse by the fact that, as you run on the treadmill with a mask over your face, struggling to breathe, a geek in a white lab coat pricks your finger every two minutes to take a blood sample to determine the red blood cell count – the higher the count the more able a person is to deliver oxygen to body tissue via the blood flow.

HOW TO PREVENT INJURIES

Every player has an Achilles heel, a repetitive injury that takes months off his career. For me it was my hamstrings, and the various teams that I've played for have come up with all manner of novel training programmes to prevent me from pulling them. From kickboxing to yoga, each programme is designed to do one thing: 'switch on' the glute muscles. Glutes (gluteus maximus) are, to be blunt, the muscles that run from your arse down towards your hamstring, and they have a fundamental flaw in that they are inherently lazy.

Footballers pull their hamstrings regularly because their glute muscles have switched off, leaving the hamstrings as the only muscles to power a player when he is sprinting and turning. As a result, the hamstrings become overworked and begin to suffer very minor muscular traumas that can, if not given enough rest, become significant tears. Tears range in severity from grade one, which can take a week or ten days to recover from, to a grade three, which is a complete tear and can, in some cases, take as long as two months to recover from.

Unfortunately, there is no one-off exercise or a switch that turns the glutes on. It has to be done each morning, and before matches, by lying on your front and training the mind to single out the muscle that you're trying to stimulate. Think of when you're trying to isolate one breast when flexing your pecks: the first time you do it, you'll tense your six-pack, your bicep and possibly the muscle in the back of your shoulder, but with enough practice you can train the mind and the body to isolate individual muscle groups.

After regular sessions the body gets the message and automatically switches on muscles – after that it is just a question of maintaining it. In truth all footballers should do this exercise every day, and not just the ones like me with dodgy hamstrings. It is estimated that players increase their anaerobic performance by as much as 20 per cent and halve the chances of pulling a hamstring, simply by using their glute muscles over their hamstrings.

But don't take my word for it, after all, I'm just a player. Let's defer to an expert, a man who has won everything in the game, and a physio who commands such huge respect that he is flown all around the world to speak about his discoveries.

The Secret Physio led a fitness and rehabilitation revolution in the Premier League – his template is still in use today by the biggest clubs in the world thanks to the sheer innovativeness of his new approach.

The Secret Footballer: *How did you work out that players should be training separately in pre-season?*

The Secret Physio: With the introduction of GPS monitoring of training and games, and systems such as Prozone, we had access to accurate data and essential statistics on players' physical and performance profiles. Those facts included the total distance covered by a player, how much distance they cover over 21 km/h or 14 km/h, how many headers they do, even whether they turn more to the left or the right during the game, and the success of certain passes. From this information it's possible to identify clearly that different positions on a football field result in different physical profiles.

For example, a centre-half may head the ball twelve times in a game but a winger not once. An attacking midfielder may cover 12 km in a game whereas a centre-half may cover less than half that distance. Therefore power- or jumping-related training is more beneficial to a centre-half, whereas the fitness training for a winger may be more sprint based. It is the same concept with goalkeepers. Goalkeepers only ever run a maximum of 15 metres in a game at any one time. They are power athletes, they need to be agile and powerful, they don't need to be aerobic or endurance athletes. Before this research, the cutting edge of a goalkeeper's fitness training was to put him in the slow group and make him do the same running as everyone else. But their fitness profile is very different to that of an outfield player. Get fit for the specific task that you want the player to achieve, not just the sport.

TSF: *Does that extend to players operating in the same position?*

The Secret Physio: Absolutely. And this is where the research began to get very interesting and really come into its own, because we realised that we were able to apply new fitness regimes to players based on the way that the manager was going to play. GPS data showed us that even players who play in the same position have different physical profiles. For example, if you were to take Patrice Evra and Luke Shaw, both are left-backs, but one does a lot more attacking and crossing from the opponents' by-line than the other, so they will cover more high-speed distance and speed endurance in a game, therefore their individual fitness training needs to reflect that. But just as important is the fact that the two players are at opposite ends of their careers, so the load that each player can take will also be different.

TSF: *So would players need to train differently from one another in terms of the weights they lift and the core work they do?*

The Secret Physio: It all depends on what you have been born with. Some players have to work on strength development in certain areas, for others it can come naturally. Let's take Lionel Messi as an example: there aren't many players who can get the ball off Messi, but it's not because he is an expert on the core-ball or can squat twice his body weight . . . his body is essentially perfectly designed to do what it needs to do to play the way he does. If there is a weakness in the system, though (say, following an injury), or if a player wants to improve an aspect of their fitness – i.e., vertical jump, or speed acceleration over 5 metres – training can improve this. And that's the big secret behind all this: essentially, what we're doing is supplementing and maximising what players have been born with. That's all it is and, when I look back now, I can't believe this wasn't understood earlier.

TSF: *In that case, every player should have an individual training programme for pre-season?*

The Secret Physio: Yes. But not just pre-season: every day of the season should be supplemented with individual instructions based on the information at hand, fitness, nutrition, sleep patterns and so on. If more coaches took 'individualised' training more literally I feel players would be more adapted and conditioned to their position, and there would be fewer injuries. Certainly when we introduced this new method at our club, one of the marked changes in the squad over that first season was that the rate of injuries dropped off. Players were no longer being told

The Secret Footballer's Guide to the Modern Game

to ask their body to perform a task that was alien to it – they were extremely comfortable doing what we told them they should be doing instead, and they thrived because of it because nobody could do it as well as they could.

There is less risk of injury when a player is more closely aligned physically and mentally to the activity he is performing. If a player does a 'new' or unaccustomed activity, problems arise. We saw it all the time when the team did a crossing and shooting session and the centre-halves and defensive midfielders joined in – they'd do twenty or thirty high-impact crosses or shots in a training session when they hardly ever did it in a game, and almost always we had cases of tight or slightly torn groins. It was the smoking gun that we'd been looking for.

In truth there was a certain amount of research already happening in American sports such as baseball and, in particular, American football. The different areas of the team all trained in smaller groups, working on their specialised tasks, before coming together as a whole team as the training progressed.

TSF: *Moving on to injuries, why does it take so long to recover from cruciate injury?*

The Secret Physio: A cruciate ligament injury occurs when the knee is forced into a position beyond the controlling capacity of the ligaments. There are two cruciate ligaments, anterior and posterior. The posterior cruciate ligament is commonly damaged in sports such as rugby and American football, when the shinbone is forced back in a collision or a scrum. With an anterior cruciate ligament injury the knee is forced inwards, together with extreme external rotation. As football relies heavily on the motion of twisting and turning, the knee has to be stable in these movements otherwise it buckles or gives way. Therefore, in football, if you rupture this ligament it will need reconstructing. If you participated in a linear sport such as cycling or even jogging, you may not need surgery, but in most ACL injuries there is also cartilage damage, so this may need rectifying too.

The operation involves taking another tissue, the graft (commonly the tendon of the patella or the hamstring from either leg), and replacing it in the same place where the original ligament would sit. As you are putting a 'tendon' in the place of a ligament, the body slowly changes the graft's cellular make-up to that of a ligament (ligamentisation) and, unfortunately, this takes time.

With more conservative surgical techniques (i.e., now the operation can all be done via an arthroscopy through two small incisions in the front of the knee rather than opening up the knee with a large incision) players can be running around after about three months. Ironically, this is actually the time when the graft is at its weakest during the recovery process. It then takes many months for the knee to gain full co-ordination and strength with a new, alien tissue inside it. The brain also needs time to readjust and relearn the complex movements of playing football. It is true that players can return in six months, but it takes many more months for them to be anywhere near where they were pre-surgery, and some surgeons still say that it takes at least nine months to return to the pitch for this very reason. All too often players return a little too soon and some players never reach their pre-injury level. The insult to the body is just too great, especially in the older player; however, young players' brains are more plastic and able to adapt to changes more quickly.

TSF: *Why do so many players pull hamstrings?*

The Secret Physio: Each sport has its own common injuries, and some clubs get more of a particular type of injury due to the type of training or style of game they've adopted. In football the common injuries are ankle sprains, knee ligament injuries, groin injuries and hamstring injuries.

The reason that we have so many hamstring injuries in football is a difficult and complex one. There are so many possible causes for hamstring injuries in a sport where an athlete is randomly sprinting, walking, turning, heading, etc. Getting older, weakness and previous injuries are the main indications for further hamstring injury.

Prevention is very challenging. However, the important aspect in the treatment stage is to focus on the main problems the player has – some find they can't sprint while others cannot consistently cut, decelerate, accelerate, twist or turn. Another problem is that so many players return when they are not fully able to cope with ninety minutes of competitive football.

TSF: *Let's talk about the World Cup. Lots of people were asking me why the England players seemed to suffer from cramp more so than almost any other team at the finals.*

The Secret Physio: Well, the Italians didn't for a few reasons, which is more about being conditioned for the climate they were playing in. Also, many of the England players hadn't played a full ninety minutes in the weeks leading up to the tournament. I don't know why they bothered going to Portugal for a week . . . they even went to St George's Park for a bit too, where the climate isn't particularly Brazilian.

There is only one answer. Get to the climate as soon as possible and teach the body to cope with the humidity and the different conditions in order for the players to adapt to the environment. The England players flew into Manaus a day or so before the game from a temperate Rio, and it was too much of a shock to their systems so they were tired and dehydrated sooner than the Italians were – that, and not being 'match fit enough' leading up to the game.

For many teams, whether you are Man United, Chelsea or the national team, the commercial side of the club can dictate the preparation for up and coming campaigns. Teams in pre-season go on long tours to Asia and the US, and England went to Portugal and Miami before getting to Brazil. Get to the venue as soon as you can to allow you time to adjust. The Germans did and they did rather well as I recall.

TSF: *And what about the rumours that the players were training in bin bags?*

The Secret Physio: It makes you dehydrate quicker because it makes you hotter and the sweat cannot evaporate. Sweat is produced to cool you down, via evaporation. But this is only part of the problem in a humid (sticky, damp) and hot environment. The air you breathe in is hot, you sweat a lot, and evaporation isn't as effective in very humid conditions. Wearing bin bags is a futile attempt to condition the body and try to cheat the conditioning process. The best way to get used to playing football at altitude in hot and humid conditions is to play football at altitude, in hot and humid conditions!

TSF: *How is it that many South American players share the same physique as their European counterparts and yet they are stronger on the ball?*

The Secret Physio: It is really noticeable how even the leanest of players, Brazilians in particular, such as Oscar, Ramires and even, before them, Ronaldinho and Cafu, seem to be far stronger on the ball than many European players. As a Premier League medical department we have been leading the research in this area for some time and we are confident that the way Brazilian players are nurtured, on uneven surfaces, particularly sand, increases their core strength enormously.

Two seasons ago we began to use sandpits for the rehabilitation of some of our players, as a sandpit works the muscles more than on grass while reducing the impact on the joints. As a player pushes off on sand the surface gives underfoot, so you need more energy to propel yourself forward, meaning that it's harder work and, by definition, players will get fitter more quickly.

Sand is particularly advantageous where joint injuries are concerned, not only because it reduces the impact on joints, but also because it protects ligaments from excessive stress and strain during rehab. When players have issues such as osteoarthritis, where the joint surfaces are worn, the sand can offer a relatively 'joint-protected' environment but also a significant muscular load. It can also be used with injuries such as ankle sprains because the ankle doesn't have to adapt and mould to a firm, uneven surface.

The pits that we use are expensive to install. Depending on size, a large pit, say 20 x 30 metres, will cost over £100,000, but through our medical and rehabilitation research we have also been able to demonstrate that using sand twice a week will benefit the whole squad, not just the injured players. They will become fitter, improve their reactions, strengthen their core and tone their physique. If I can offer one piece of advice to any person reading this book who is trying to reach their peak physical condition, it would be to try to incorporate sand training into your regime – the benefits are huge.

TSF: *What ideas are being worked on to revolutionise the medical set-up with the England team?*

The Secret Physio: One of the glaringly poor areas between national teams (although England are better than most) and clubs is the lack of respect, communication and trust between medical personnel. I admire the rugby set-up, where England physios are welcomed into clubs to assist and advise on the wellbeing of a player and even help out with their rehab and recovery at times. I know the England rugby players' situation is contractually different to football, and that many football clubs feel a sense of ownership and lack of control at having an 'outsider' come into the club but, come on, let's get professional about this. Unlike many other aspects of football, the medical staff are bound to rules of confidentiality and professional conduct. And, after all, don't we all have the best interests of the player at heart?

The whole England set-up needs refreshing. The playing squad is going to be made up of young players, so let's have a dynamic ethos, forward-thinking medical and performance personnel and player wellbeing strategies at national level that will be the envy of other sports. Look at how other elite sporting organisations, such as Team Sky and British Cycling, work. They do not leave any stone unturned when looking for ways of improving performance and solving a problem, even in small amounts – they call it 'marginal gains'. For example, they realised that when on a Grand Tour the riders were in a different hotel bed every night and not getting a great night's sleep between stages. Sleep is the best recovery you can get, so they ensured that each rider's bed had its own individual topper, pillow and duvet. Now every bed is the same and they get a proper night's sleep. Simple, really.

TSF: *Are foreign players generally fitter?*

The Secret Physio: Not at all, that is a myth. The adage that foreign players have come to the Premier League and showed us the way in terms of fitness and nutrition was true once, but not now. That doesn't mean we can't still learn from new ideas coming over from the Continent, but I know that in the Premier League today, although there are more foreign players, everyone is fit. English players play far less golf than they used to years ago, and they look after themselves better – they have to in order to compete at Premier League level; there is no alternative to the proper lifestyle in today's game. Today, the game is faster, more intense and if you have cup competitions you play fifty to sixty games per season. You have to be fit.

In my view, the foreign players tend to hang around more after training as there are fewer distractions in a foreign country, and this can mean that they do additional gym-related work, have more massages, etc. Some say it's being more professional, some say it's higher maintenance. But English players aren't out drinking buckets of beer in the meantime; they are at home resting, doing what professional players should be doing.

TSF: *What is the budget for a physio or medical department?*

The Secret Physio: This varies massively – from clubs such as Manchester City, who will spend millions on medical-related costs, to a few hundred thousand at your lower Championship side.

The biggest cost is wages, which will obviously depend on staff numbers and experience. For example, we have a number of doctors, physios, masseurs, admin staff and so on. The bigger clubs have up to fifteen full-time medical staff, whereas a League One club may only have one full-time physio. Then there are the costs of scans and operations, seeing specialists at home and abroad, where the cost skyrockets. Then there are electrical physio treatment machines, rehab equipment, hydrotherapy and pool facilities that cost big money to install and maintain. And you've also got the day-to-day products, such as tape, oils, dressings, drugs, etc. At a top Champions League club, you could easily be looking at a bill of £6 million or £7 million a year.

TSF: *Can you explain your relationship with the manager?*

The Secret Physio: The relationship between manager and physio varies enormously between clubs. I have worked with managers in the past so closely that they become close friends, while there were others that I hardly spoke to from day to day. When you are the only medical person at a club you will obviously have a very close working relationship with the manager. You will be discussing issues regarding both fit and injured players, numerous times in a day.

At bigger clubs it is important to have one person who is directly responsible for discussing these medical issues with the manager. If too many people get involved things get complicated and misinterpreted. This person is usually the head of medicine, who can be a doctor, as is the case at clubs like Man City and Liverpool, or a club can be physio-led, as is the case at Arsenal and Tottenham. In an ideal world every member of staff would have an input into a player's management, but it is the head of the department who discusses it with the manager.

Some managers think they are medically trained and want to give advice on how the injured player should be managed. On one occasion my manager was insisting a player play with a skullcap to cover a deep cut on his head. Trouble was, he couldn't head the ball properly. It turned out that he was fine with just a bit of padding and strapping. The player was very relieved not to play with a helmet on.

TSF: *Do you get pressure to rush players back, or are you left alone and trusted?*

The Secret Physio: Generally no [to rushing players back]. The manager knows and trusts our department to do our very best to get a player fit and with minimal risk of re-injury as soon as possible. Good injury management involves regular communication with the manager and updates on a player's progress. Managers don't like surprises. When their star striker is out injured, of course they want him back as quickly as possible, as do we, but it is working out a balance of being fully fit to perform and minimising risk of re-injury which extends the recovery period further. Re-injuries should be avoided as much as possible. They take longer to heal and indicate that a player wasn't ready to return to play.

TSF: *Are some players a nightmare to deal with?*

The Secret Physio: Footballers are human beings, and the great thing about humans is their diversity. Some players have a low pain threshold and whinge at the slightest blister or niggle, whereas others will play on with a broken leg, literally. Some are used to massages twice a day and have to be supervised to carry out a gym programme, whereas other players you never see on the massage table and you will never see them unless it's a really serious problem.

That's also why, when you cover a game, you have to know your players. There are those players who go down a lot but are usually fine, and those who rarely stay down injured, and if they do you know it's serious.

TSF: *Finally, the question that I get asked more than any other by kids up and down the country at the minute. Does that multicoloured tape that players wear all over their skin actually do anything?*

The Secret Physio: As with most medical treatments, it works for some people and not for others. If you believe that wearing the tape is going to make you feel better, it usually will; if you don't believe in it, then it probably won't work. It's the same with acupuncture, Pilates . . . most electrical machines. The tape is supposed to provide support or release tension in the soft tissue it covers. It is also believed to affect the pain input to the brain, which eases discomfort, but this may be very subtle. Does it matter whether you wear pink, blue, black or beige? Whatever makes you 'feel' better!

Diet, nutrition and supplements

There is always research going on into certain areas of human phenomena that can perhaps be applied to football nutrition and fitness in order to gain a slight advantage. For example, in recent years there has been a lot of research into why a certain village in France called Bach, about an hour north of Toulouse, should have the lowest rate of heart disease and the longest life span in the whole of France. Known as the 'French paradox', the people of this region eat more saturated fat, thanks to their love of foods like cheese and confit of duck, than in any other part of the country. Dated research can sometimes be to blame for turning a whole country off saturated fats or sugars, and it's true that too much saturated fat does indeed clog the arteries around the heart – but we now know that, as part of a varied diet, saturated fat in moderation is actually a vital part of living a healthy life.

Very often, however, there is a more sinister marketing ploy behind whole generations of people taking up one eating habit or another.

For example, research into where the 'eight glasses of water a day' advice came from has shown that it was directly linked to a marketing strategy developed by a French natural mineral water company in order to sell more water. The reality is that there is very little evidence to suggest that a magic number of eight glasses of water a day is any better than drinking six or twelve, or any other number in between for that matter. And marketing like this isn't a new thing – the notion that eating five portions of fruit and veg a day will greatly increase immunity to certain deadly diseases has also since been shown to be nothing more than a gimmick developed by the EU parliament to boost agricultural productivity and sales of fruit and veg. Two years ago, they upped it to seven portions. No one is saying that you shouldn't eat fruit and veg or drink water – only that we should all be aware of when we are being healthy, and when we are being sold to.

That said, there are a lot of things regarding nutrition that we do know to be a matter of fact, and some of them seem to fly in the face of modern 'advice'. Dark chocolate (over 74 per cent cocoa solids) is one of the best things for you. In the Premier League we eat two squares every morning as part of a very rigid diet. The sacrifice that goes into our diets is considerable; depending on where you live good food is all around you, and so is every temptation that the biggest food manufacturers on the planet can think of. But, if you want to live your life like a Premier League footballer in terms of the foods you should eat, then below is exactly what you need to eat and when.

THE DIET – IN SEASON

8.30 a.m.–9 a.m.: One Actimel, one pint of lukewarm water with the juice of half a lemon, two small squares of dark chocolate (minimum 74 per cent cocoa).

The Actimel helps to increase more of the bacteria that break down food, thus speeding up metabolism. The pint of water must be lukewarm because the body will use energy to heat ice-cold water to body temperature, so that it can be absorbed into warm muscles without chilling them. The lemon juice helps to increase metabolism speed – important so that sugars reach muscles faster as the foods are broken down more quickly. When we are training at a high tempo this becomes a fundamentally important part of our diet.

9.30 a.m.: Two slices of brown toast with almond spread. You may also try porridge with honey for a change.

White bread is one of the worst foods that any person can eat – it is pumped full of chemicals to increase the life span of the bread. Brown bread is far more natural, with very few additives. Nuts are a so-called 'super food' but, most importantly where footballers and athletes are concerned, they are a slow-releasing energy source. This means that if a player is training solidly for two hours, the energy levels within his muscles are continually being topped up by the energy coming from the nuts.

10.30 a.m.–12.30 p.m.: Training.
1 p.m.: Steamed broccoli, grilled chicken (no skin), lots of brown rice.

I don't just mean a couple of florets of broccoli either. I mean six to eight florets. Brown rice has replaced pasta because it has recently been found that nearly a third of all players have some kind of food intolerance, and the egg in the pasta was actually hindering their performance. The skin on chicken, although extremely tasty, is very bad for you and so it is removed. What remains is a big lump of unseasoned protein. The chicken is grilled to avoid using fat, and the broccoli is steamed to retain as many nutrients as possible. On the Continent, the lubrication comes from olive oil, but over here we think of Queen and country and go in dry.

Nutrition

In season

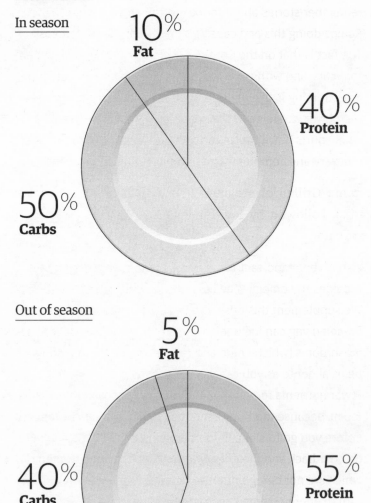

10% **Fat**

40% **Protein**

50% **Carbs**

Out of season

5% **Fat**

40% **Carbs**

55% **Protein**

The reason for that is because most managers have now banned ketchup from the club dining room. You may remember stories about former Tottenham manager Juande Ramos doing this and causing some ripples in the process. The fact is that on the Continent ketchup has been banished for years, and with good reason: eating a sachet of ketchup after training is like eating a cube of sugar, meaning that the player would get a sharp energy spike followed by what sports nutritionists call a 'crash'. In short, it doesn't aid recovery and completely messes with your body's wellbeing.

6 p.m.: Grilled or steamed fish with steamed veg (avoid carbs). Followed by low-fat yogurt and fruit – berries in particular.

Fish is very important in a footballer's diet because it provides the omega-3 oils essential for the body's wellbeing. We supplement this dose of omega-3 heavily (see page 33). Steamed veg can include any kind of veg you like, as well as mushrooms (which I hate and refuse to eat). The veg should be as al dente as you can stand – the more cooking, the fewer nutrients remain. Avoid having too many carbs after 6 p.m. because the body cannot absorb them in the time left before you go to sleep, by which point you will be lying flat on your back and the energy from the carbs you've eaten, which are not being burnt through training and exercise, will turn to energy stores, otherwise known as fat!

Snacks: Raw vegetables – a bag of baby carrots is perfect.

At Manchester City's training ground, the breakdown of nutrition needed is individually tailored and written on a wall for each player, changing from day to day, depending on whether or not the players need more or less of a particular food group according to their training regime. It is all designed to have the players in the best condition they can be in for Saturday.

MATCH DAY

Match day is very different from any other day of the week. Half the time you will be at the mercy of the hotel's chef, who very often is a man who lost his love for cooking long, long ago. That said, there are only so many variations of chicken, rice and pasta that somebody can conjure up.

Generally, we'll eat a breakfast at around 8 or 9 a.m. of muesli and cereal, but never anything sugary, to make sure we avoid the dreaded crash. Then there is a pre-match meal at about 11.30, after a walk and before a team meeting in which we watch a video of the opposition as a refresher and have a bit of a rallying cry from the coaching team. The pre-match meal must be as plain as possible to avoid upsetting the stomach, and generally consists of boiled penne with a sauce made by opening cans of tinned tomatoes and heating the contents up. Then there is grilled chicken, not seasoned, and a selection of steamed veg. And that's it.

At half-time we have a table of slow-releasing sugar foods. The most popular are Jaffa Cakes and jelly babies, but at some clubs these have been replaced by concentrated gels designed to get into the bloodstream more quickly, deliver a bigger hit and last longer. At Arsenal the players are given a sugar cube, which is left to dissolve on their tongue. But I think that may be because they are often making a concerted effort to storm the first fifteen minutes of the second half, a time in which Arsenal have typically been at their strongest.

For many years (and still at certain clubs to this day), it has been a widely held belief that after each match in which a player has played at least sixty minutes, he can eat whatever he likes. When I started playing professionally, fish and chips was the undisputed king of post-match cuisine. Today it's pizza, delivered straight to the changing room, while at the highest level the chef on board the coach ride home will typically cook a pasta Bolognese or a carbonara. At one team I played for we used to have a heated-up low-fat muffin with low-fat custard and, believe me, we savoured every mouthful, it was the one treat of the week.

SUPPLEMENTS

At every stage of a player's diet, he'll be boosting his vitamin levels and intake of protein with a selection of pre-approved supplements 'prescribed' by the club's nutritionist. Below is a selection of the staple products that pretty much all footballers will take in some guise or another.

Cod liver oil: Some players take as many as ten tablets a day, but you must be careful as cod liver oil is where we get our healthy dose of fatty acids. Exceeding the recommended daily amount can have an adverse effect. Leading scientists across the globe who research anti-ageing effects all agree that the one proven thing that every person can do to extend their life span is to take daily doses of cod liver oil.

Caffeine tablets: Only to be taken on a match day. I hate them – all they do for me is keep me awake after the match has finished, but I know lots of players who swear by them and who claim that the tablets make them more alert during the game. I call them placebo tablets.

Creatine: Taken on the Continent for years, for a long time creatine was seen as a banned substance in this country and has had lots of negative press. What I can tell you, from years of taking it, is that the creatine from over ten years ago was extremely pure and the effects were noticeable. I felt much stronger in training and able to recover much faster. I could lift weights beyond anything that I thought I was capable of, and I seemed to be faster in a flat race. Creatine was never banned, but it is something that has been honed over the years, and today you tend to find it in protein shakes rather than a powder to be mixed in with water and downed. But that may be because it tastes revolting on its own.

Maximuscle: Maximuscle shakes are one brand of quick carb- and protein-based products that can deliver the required amount of nutrition to a player's system quickly. In truth, there are many products all doing the same thing. The reason shakes have taken over in the game is because they can be pre-made and kept on ice until the players have finished training. There is a rule of thumb that players must take in the energy that has been expended within thirty minutes of physical activity, otherwise the body struggles to replenish its stocks effectively. But players were coming off the training pitch and getting showered, checking their phones and waiting around for lunch, so the shakes have provided the perfect antidote. These days players will be handed their own bottles of pre-mixed protein shake, usually with a dose of creatine mixed in, as they are walking off the training pitch and still in their boots.

Drinks: Players in the Premier League will have little choice but to drink Lucozade – even if you prefer Red Bull or Powerade, and buy your own to drink in the warm-up, you'll find that your club will be fined a big sum of money by the Premier League. Only Lucozade can be consumed on the pitch in the Premier League, thanks to their lucrative sponsorship deal. You could, of course, put a different drink in those blue Lucozade bottles by the side of the dugouts, but why bother? Lucozade is actually a very good drink to hydrate with, as good as anything else that's out there. Just try to use the pop-up nozzle on the bottle, or a straw, when you drink it, otherwise your teeth will be shot to pieces by the time you've been in the game a decade or longer. Also, there is no need whatsoever to drink any sports drinks when you're at home – just drink water unless you want to do what Samuel Eto'o does, and just drink Coca-Cola, morning, noon and night. Coke is one of the worst things that anybody can put into their body, but Samuel doesn't seem to have done badly off it.

HOW DOES A PLAYER MAKE ALL THIS WORK FOR HIM?

Every player will at some point sit down with a nutritionist who scrutinises everything that they do off the pitch and how the level of performance can be improved. Some players have vitamin deficiencies that need to be supplemented and some players are carrying too much body fat. At Fulham, like at so many clubs I know, there was a real competition to see who could get the lowest body fat with some of the players achieving sub-5 per cent, which I have to tell you is very impressive. How they achieved it is a testament to the nutrition and fitness staff and the attention to detail that went in to each player's individualised programme.

Below is an example of a typical nutritional programme, taken from a real Premier League player, showing the level of detail required to help a top player to stay at his peak:

BIO SIGNATURES:
Body fat   – 7.1 %
Weight   – 76.2 kg
Lean mass – 70.8 kg

DEFICIENCIES:
Vitamin C
Vitamin D
Magnesium
Folate (B9)
Pancreatic enzymes
High mercury

FOOD INTOLERANCES:
Cow's milk, blackcurrants

INTERVENTION:
Eat according to the FFC nutrition guide
Eat more green vegetables, beans and legumes (sources of folate and B vitamins)
Vary fruits and vegetables
Reduce shellfish and tuna consumption (high levels of mercury)
Eat nuts (almonds, walnuts and pistachios) and seeds (magnesium)

SUPPLEMENTS:

Pre-training	*Post-training*	*As advised*
Vitamin D: 5 tabs	Calm down:	Magnesium: 4 tabs in the
Create-alanine:	4 tabs*	evening
4 tabs		Fish oils: 4 with meals
		Digestaid: 1 with meals
		Chlorella: 4 tabs

OTHER TIPS

☺ Avoid red meat if you can, but particularly after Wednesdays, when the body cannot digest it in time before a match on a Saturday – and that leads to a feeling of sluggishness and fatigue during the game.

☺ Always take an ice bath after every training session, and especially after a match. The icy water stops any bleeding in the leg muscles which can lead to strains and tears. Most clubs use wheelie bins filled with ice water and leave them outside the changing rooms; others will have the youth team fill baths for the first team and others will have specialist plunge pools installed in the training complex.

☺ Most clubs will test you for food intolerance. But if for any reason they don't then the club doctor can arrange it. And it's well worth doing: 35 per cent of the British population has a food intolerance of some description and the level of performance on the pitch can be affected severely depending on the severity. A player I played with for years took a food intolerance test and found that he had a really

---

* 'Calm down' is a term used to describe multiple tablets which, when taken together, have the effect of calming the player down after all the tablets he took to get himself up before the game. These tablets would contain phosphorylated serine (which suppresses cortisol and makes the happy hormone serotonin) and phosphatidryl choline (a fat that makes good hormones).

bad aversion to dairy that made him tired. Once he had cut dairy out of his diet he was like a new man. Some of the more cynical players in the squad claimed it was nothing more than a placebo, but it worked, so who cares?

☹ Sleep is the most important requirement for good recovery and recovery is the most important thing off the pitch. Recovery is the buzzword of the moment and we're only really now understanding its importance. What we do know is that sleep plays a vital part in the process. Certain foods can help to aid a good night's rest (see below). This can also be supplemented with other sleep aids, such as ensuring that you have a very dark room, getting a very high-quality bed with a Tempur mattress and turning off all electronic equipment well before you go to bed: iPads, phones and TV stimulate the brain, which is the opposite of what you want to happen.

THREE THINGS YOUR BODY NEEDS TO PRODUCE FOR A GOOD SLEEP AND THE FOODS THAT CONTAIN THEM

Tryptophan	Serotonin	Melatonin
Prawns and fish (salmon, tuna, cod)	Salmon, fresh tuna, snapper, sardines, mackerel, halibut	Pineapples, bananas, raspberries, cherries
Turkey	Walnuts, flaxseeds, pumpkin seeds, sesame seeds, almonds	Oats and rice
Cashews, almonds, walnuts	Omega-3, chlorella, spirulina	Sweetcorn, tomatoes,
Lentils, black beans, kidney beans	Brown rice and eggs	Ginger

IN SUMMARY

This isn't a cookbook; it's simply a guide to the level of dedication and sacrifice needed to succeed in this game. It also shows you that there is a relentless quest for those 'winning margins' that could make a difference – everybody associated with football is continually on the lookout for those. Of course you can add herbs and spices to your chicken, of course you can have lentils instead of boiled rice and, yes, it won't kill you if you have jelly and ice cream for pudding on a Monday instead of low-fat yogurt and fruit but, in the main, what you have just read is exactly what the top-level players give the best years of their lives to. It isn't a lot of fun, and no amount of money will ever make steamed broccoli taste any different, but it is a true reflection, so far as diet and fitness is concerned, of what is required to succeed as a Premier League footballer.

And if you do succumb to the power of marketing and find that you just can't resist a Big Mac and fries any longer, do yourself a favour and don't splash it all over Instagram, as one of my old teammates did. Unless, of course, you don't mind paying a week's money as a fine. Personally, I'd stick to boiled rice, it's healthier and cheaper.

Equipment

Of course, nutrition, fitness and injury prevention are only part of the story. The top clubs will also invest everything they have in the latest training-ground technology to give them the edge – and they are aided by manufacturers and

HOW DO YOU TAKE A FREE-KICK LIKE RONALDO?

In 1908 Major League Baseball pitcher Eddie Cicotte, of the Chicago White Sox, noticed a variation in the performance of the ball depending on how he held it and how it left his grip. In particular, Cicotte found that if he gripped the ball between his knuckles before releasing it he could remove the spin from a pitch, and when that happened the ball behaved in a bizarre way – it wobbled.

But it wasn't fancy equipment that initially drove the refinement of Cicotte's discovery; it was about understanding what was happening to the ball once it left its origin – it is a matter of physics.

Without applying any spin to a pitch, a ball is left to cut through the natural drag of the air around it. The undulations around the stitching of a ball disrupt the airflow and the ball's natural path and, as the ball speeds up, the forces become greater as the air reacts against the stitching more violently – and this, ultimately, affects a ball's trajectory. The air moves up over the stitching and comes back down the other side, pushing the ball down; but the air underneath the ball does the same and pushes the ball back up. This force also works from side to side depending on how the ball is released. The forces acting against each other make a ball wobble up and down which, in turn, makes it incredibly difficult for any batsman to judge the flight. Cicotte called the pitch 'knuckleball', and in football we call it 'the wobbler'. But on the Continent it

external companies only too happy to oblige with cutting-edge technology of their own.

is known as 'knuckleballing' – it seems that the Americans have always been the experts when it comes to branding.

The first time I saw a player use the technique in a football match was before Ronaldo's time. Juninho Pernambucano was a Brazilian international who began his career in 1993, but made his name with the fantastic Lyon side between 2001 and 2009, during which time the French club won seven consecutive championships. Juninho scored 75 competitive goals for Lyon, 44 of them from direct free-kicks, including four from a distance measured at 40 yards or more.

The good news is that anybody can do it; the technique needed to replicate a wobbling free-kick is simply a question of practice and a little bit of know-how, which I'll share with you now. For a long time, players tried to copy others like Juninho and, later, Ronaldo, by kicking the ball from

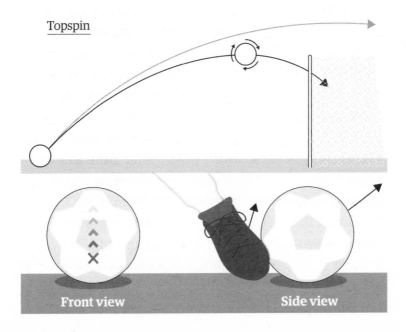

Topspin

Front view   Side view

bottom to top and trying to put as much topspin on the ball as possible in order to get the required dip. What resulted was a new type of free-kick that didn't wobble but went straight up and down very quickly. It was popularised by Didier Drogba, and can be seen today thanks to players like Paris Saint-Germain's David Luiz, who struck a beautiful free-kick for Brazil against Colombia in the 2014 World Cup, and Wigan's Shaun Maloney, who scored a perfect example against Arsenal at the Emirates Stadium in 2013. These guys have taken it to a new level because we now know that to put more topspin on the ball, we need to hit it with a bigger surface area of our foot, so, rather than just using the big toe, we use a full side foot and kick up the ball, from bottom to top.

Technically, however, the knuckleball free-kick is a little more difficult to pull off consistently. I have witnessed the best exponents hit five perfect free-kicks, only to hit the next five all over the training ground. The reason for this is that a player only uses his big toe, which means that if he doesn't strike the ball exactly in the sweet spot then he is just as likely to pull the shot to the left as he is to find the goal. In fact, it is easy to spot a player who can't execute the free-kick properly, because the shots nearly always end up fading to the left after barely getting into the air. In short, it is very easy to look like a poor player when trying to execute this free-kick – perhaps that's why Ronaldo always claims that the wall is too close or that there is a hand-ball whenever he miskicks one.

The correct way to take a knuckleball free-kick is to run at the ball straighter than you normally would and strike it just above the equator, usually with your big toe, and with

The knuckleball free-kick

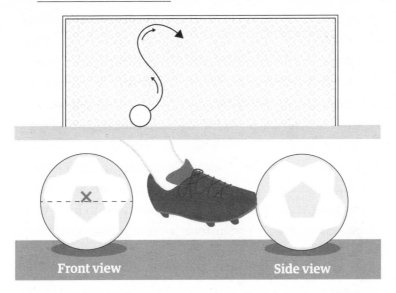

Front view   Side view

as much force as you can muster, depending on how close you are to the goal, of course. The big-toe rule is not set in stone; Andrea Pirlo, the legendary Italian playmaker, said in his book that he felt three toes under the ball worked best for him. It isn't an exact science – players have different-sized feet and different styles of striking a ball, dependent on their dominant muscles. The point being, if you can't do it off one toe, don't just give up, because there is no reason why, with a bit of experimentation, you won't be able to nail the correct technique.

Once you've found your own particular variation, physics takes over. The ball contracts as the energy from the kick is transferred to it, and the air inside becomes compressed before snapping back again, creating a pulsating effect. It's this effect that causes the air around the ball to run around it in a bizarre way, similar to how the stitching affects a baseball – the grooves between the panelling act as a carefully designed channel for the air to maximise the effect. The result is a wobble.

These days sports manufacturers are very keen for every professional player to be able to do this, because it's harder for goalkeepers to save, and, after all, every player is a potential hero. Millions are spent on ball technology to make sure that the panelling is laid out in a way that will encourage the air to run through the channels more irregularly to make the ball wobble more violently. For many years the panelling on a football had a regular hexagonal layout but, today, if you put a Nike football and an Adidas football next to one another you'll see that the panelling is distinct, even though both are FIFA approved. The Nike ball is used in the Premier League, La Liga and Serie A; while the Adidas ball was used throughout the 2014 World Cup.

When I was a kid, a new Mitre football, which was the ball used in the top division, cost my mum £10, but the huge outlay of Adidas and Nike to determine the best way to construct a football, purely to aid the way it moves through the air, now means that the price of a Nike Incyte ball costs £99.99, while the Adidas Brazuca World Cup ball was priced at £113 on its release, a 1030 per cent mark-up on its 24-year-old predecessor. Not quite the $50,000 paid for a signed 1919 World Series baseball, but maybe if eight FIFA delegates signed a World Cup ball when the Qatar World Cup comes around, we might be able to nudge the asking price upwards in a few years.

But sports manufacturers do not spend millions of pounds developing a product unless there is a market for it. In June 2014, Adidas revealed a new 'smart ball' with built-in sensors that, with the aid of the company's miCoach app via Bluetooth, can monitor the speed of a ball, the impact point and the flight trajectory. The fact that it was on sale in Apple stores only goes to show the direction that football is heading. The goal is to help players to learn faster and become more consistent when practising penalties and free-kicks. Ultimately, it will help to increase the number of players two who can replicate every type of free-kick in the professional game, but, at £250, you've got to really want to take free-kicks like Ronaldo.

It's all a long way from the humble beginnings of knuckleball, but money has always talked. Eddie Cicotte is perhaps less well known for his pioneering discovery than he is infamous for his involvement in baseball's biggest match-fixing scandal when, in 1919, eight White Sox players threw the World Series, losing to the unfancied Cincinnati Reds. That White Sox team are now known as the Black Sox and, although Cicotte and his seven teammates were acquitted in court, they were all banned from baseball for life.

WHERE DOES THAT LEAVE GOALKEEPERS?

So many goalkeeping coaches I know have tried to develop their own glove or a training aid they can then bring to market. It is pointless in that there is no money in it whatsoever. The best way for a goalkeeping coach to make extra money would be to run courses in the summer, or continually bring in young goalkeepers on trial in the hope of finding a good one he can then become the agent for.

Despite that, it doesn't seem to stop them from putting in huge amounts of time and cash in the hope of having their very own Dyson moment. There is a huge range of products on the market for goalkeepers, more than for outfield players. You might think that a position in which only a few people can play wouldn't lend itself to having so many products but, actually, that is precisely the reason there are so many. They are specialised products that are either cheap – like the ball that looks as if it has Toblerones sticking out of it, which is used when practising shots that bounce just before the keeper to improve his reactions – or not-so-cheap, like the £13,000 machine that can replicate a Ronaldo free-kick.

A guy turned up with one at our training ground not so long ago. He had developed it, and was taking it to professional clubs in the hope of selling it, having rather astutely worked out that no goalkeeping coach could replicate a Ronaldo free-kick. He unveiled his machine in front of a suitably impressed audience of players and switched it on. He pointed it at the goal, from roughly 40 yards out, and began feeding balls between two spinning discs of different speeds. The discs squeezed the balls between them and fired them one at a time out the other side. The maximum speed of the machine was 90 miles per hour, and the balls moved all over the place.

Needless to say, we all took a turn in goal to see exactly why these goalkeepers make such a fuss about free-kicks. When it was my turn, I slipped the gloves on. The first shot I honestly didn't see, I only heard it. The ball smashed off the crossbar with such force that the makeshift goal retreated on its wheels by a foot. If the ball had hit me in the face it would have broken my nose and knocked me out.

Aside from certain death, there was one other major drawback with that particular machine. When we'd finished messing around with it, the discs had shredded the balls to pieces and, although every club gets a quota of free balls at the start of the year and then another quota of yellow balls when the winter period kicks in, a club is obliged to buy any extra balls that it needs. While £1000 isn't a lot of money for a Premier League club to pay out for another bag of ten balls, it soon adds up for lower-league teams, who certainly wouldn't want to be paying that every week just so a goalkeeper can practise repelling free-kicks.

It was a shame in a way because, as I've said, no goalkeeping coach I know can replicate a Ronaldo free-kick, and the more kids who are attempting to learn how to nail the technique needed to pull one off, the more goalkeepers are going to have to work out how to stop the wobbler.

The goals that influenced me most

Let me say at the start that choosing a definitive 'best of' list for anything is tough, but to do that for goals is impossible unless you set out a few ground rules. The goals listed below are the ones that have influenced me more than any others. Some of them are the goals that have made me want to finish my dinner as quickly as possible, go over the park, wrap the swings behind their posts and

47

practise them until it was so dark that my mum called me back in. Some of the more recent ones are the goals that I show to the young attacking players coming through the various academies of the teams I have played for. They are the benchmark for the skills that are on show, whether that skill is passing and moving, technical manipulation of the ball or how to play within a team while still being an individual. They are all great goals but, then again, I could write an entire book on my favourite goals, and the list on each page would be different from the last.

Neymar, Santos v Flamengo, Brazilian Serie A, 2011

 Santos went 3–0 up, the third of which came from a ridiculous run from Neymar. He picked the ball up on the wing and produced a dazzling piece of footwork to jink between two Flamengo players before coming in off the line and reversing the ball into a front man and receiving a 'wall pass' back. He has the strength to hold off a midfielder and run directly at the exposed centre-half as he takes the return pass in his stride. The next part is what makes the goal. He somehow drags his foot over the ball but nudges it past the defender with his other foot as he does so, before running around the other side of the centre-half and collecting the ball again. Neymar is ever so slightly off balance as the goalkeeper comes out to close him down and has to strike the ball with the outside of his right foot, but he is still able to lift the ball over the keeper's body so as to avoid any chance that the keeper might get a touch and ruin, what is for me, one of the most skilful goals I've ever seen. There is just one problem: in the second half, Santos capitulate in their own stadium and somehow contrive to lose the game 4–5. The player with a hat trick for Flamengo? The legendary Ronaldinho.

Lionel Messi, Barcelona v Getafe, Spanish league, 2007

 Lionel Messi was just nineteen when he scored a goal that would be compared to Diego Maradona's solo effort against England in the 1986 World Cup quarter-final. The Barcelona dribbler picks the ball up in his own half on the right wing and beats two men before sprinting off towards the opposition goal. He outpaces the two players he's just beaten and approaches the penalty area, where two defenders lunge at him. He dribbles through the middle of them before rounding the goalkeeper and lifting the ball over the body of a despairing defender sliding in on the line. Personally, with the possible exception of Ryan Giggs, I haven't seen too many players do that at the age of nineteen, in a top-flight game for one of the biggest teams in the world.

Lionel Messi, Barcelona v Real Sociedad, Spanish league, 2010

 Tiki-taka at its finest. Barcelona are already 2–0 up and have kept the ball for nearly a minute by the time Lionel Messi takes a return pass in his stride and slots it past the keeper. The scary part about this goal is that Real Sociedad are really trying to win the ball back from Barcelona, they are on the front foot and pressing them in an attempt to force a mistake. The move that leads to the goal is an exhibition of passing and moving. It starts on the right wing, where Xavi, Dani Alves and Messi are exchanging passes under pressure, and ends with Messi and Alves swapping the ball all the way up the pitch until Messi scores. The move features nearly twenty passes, eight of which are one-touch, and there are a remarkable six one-twos between Messi and Alves. Keep your eye on Dani Alves because in this one move he features as a right-back, a centre midfielder and a number 9.

Arie Haan, Holland v Italy, World Cup, second round, 1978

 When I was a kid I had a video of every World Cup up to 1986. On that tape was this goal by Arie Haan, the first long-range strike that stuck in my head. A huge number of fantastic goals have been scored from distance before and since, but this was the one that, as a kid, I tried to copy. He also repeated the feat against Germany at the same World Cup.

Years later I met Haan when, for reasons that were never clear, he turned up at our training ground with his World Cup medal and began talking to the lads about his career. They say that you should never meet your heroes, but Haan was an exception – he was such a humble man and had great banter to boot.

Haan is, understandably, eclipsed outside of Holland by Johan Cruyff, but consider this: Haan played in two consecutive World Cup finals, in 1974 and 1978 (losing both), while winning 35 caps for Holland. And he was a member of the legendary Ajax team that won three consecutive European Cups from 1971 to 1973, three league titles, three Dutch Cups and an Intercontinental Cup. That haul includes one double, one treble and one quadruple. When he moved to the Belgian club, Anderlecht, he won the league once, the cup, two UEFA Cups and two UEFA Super Cups. And you thought Ronaldo was a good player.

Nelinho, Brazil v Italy, World Cup third-place play-off, 1978

 I remember the first time that I saw this goal. It was on the same FIFA World Cup VHS as Arie Haan's strike and was unlike anything I had seen before. I'd never seen any player bend the ball with the outside of his foot like this, not least from the corner of the box, which is where Brazilian right-back, Nelinho, hits it from. It was always said of any goal that if Dino Zoff, the legendary Italian goalkeeper, couldn't save it, then nobody could. In fairness, Liam Brady scored one like this in 1978 against Tottenham, but that was a little more central and had slightly less bend on it. Even so, it was on my tape and I tried to replicate it with limited success.

And there are other elements to Nelinho's goal that make it very watchable. As a little kid, crackly commentary gave the World Cup that distant quality – you were watching something happening far away in a new and exciting country. Listening to that today gives goals and clips like this a very nostalgic feel, romantic even. I'm all for progress but, to me at least, thanks to the uniform advertising, the fact that we now see the players on our TVs every week, and the sharpness of the TV production, every game in the World Cup at every modern-day tournament always feels as if it's being played in one universal stadium. Today, the World Cup has a very generic feel about it – the idiosyncrasies of playing in a tournament in, say, Italy in 1990, with its individual style from city to city, are gone, for the time being. Brazil built a raft of new stadiums for the 2014 World Cup, Russia will build a raft of new stadiums in 2018 and Qatar will build new stadiums and cities in 2022, and all of those stadiums will look and feel much the same as one another.

As a side note, I know that people will point to the free-kick that Roberto Carlos scored against France as the ultimate example of a goal scored using nothing more than the laws of the Magnus effect, but in my list you get points for being the first. I give you former Cruzeiro player, Geraldão.

Matt Le Tissier, Southampton v Newcastle, 1993

Southampton legend Le Tissier had a reputation for scoring exquisite goals, and when I really got into watching *Match of the Day* as a kid, the goal of the month award was certain to feature a Matt Le Tissier strike. He was the first player who I saw flick the ball up from a free-kick and volley it over the wall. But his finest goal, in my opinion, came against Newcastle in 1993. It is so skilful that it deserves to grace most lists. The three touches he takes to get the ball under control while beating a defender at the same time are by no means easy and all have to be perfect. I later read that the slightly scuffed finish had taken the gloss off it for

Le Tissier himself, but, for me, it serves as a lesson in composure in front of goal for every kid who wants to be a striker.

Zlatan Ibrahimović, Ajax v NAC, 2004

He's not my cup of tea, Ibrahimović, I'm afraid, but in football he is loved by the players: they love his cockiness and the comments that he comes out with pertaining to his own talent. I find it quite distasteful and can see why he has changed clubs so many times. However, the man can score a great goal, there's no denying that, and in my view this is his best. He picks the ball up with his back to goal and actually has a poor first touch before rescuing the situation with sheer strength against an opponent who tries to take it off him. From that point there is no stopping him; he wriggles and twists and turns and dummies his way into the penalty area, feigning to shoot three times and leaving eight players (some more than once) and a goalkeeper in his wake. I love this goal, I don't like him.

Dennis Bergkamp, Newcastle v Arsenal, 2002

Any kid out there who wants to know how important a first touch is in football should study videos of Dennis Bergkamp. He scored his fair share of goals but he created so many with a one-touch pass or a quick chop one way and an incisive through-ball in the opposite direction. He had a total understanding of where everybody was on the pitch, both his own team and the opposition. This goal shows Bergkamp at his very best and marks him out as technically superlative.

Almost any other player I have seen would try to control the horrible bouncing ball that comes into him. But Bergkamp, with his back to goal, flicks it one side of the defender and runs the other, before using his strength to outmuscle the defender and find the calmest of finishes. For a long time, some people debated whether or not Dennis had actually intended to do what he did here. Like so many others, those people don't truly understand football.

THE ART OF WAR
How to Put a Winning Team Together

'If you know the enemy and know yourself, you need not fear the results of a hundred battles'

Sun Tzu

At the start of every season a manager will study each section of the league depending on where he thinks his team will finish. He needs to know how many goals he will have to score and how many he can afford to concede. Then he works out where he wants his goals to come from and which style of football he will play in order to make it happen. He does all this by studying the Premier League table over the course of about five seasons to determine what the average is.

You might think that a manager simply has to look at how many games he has to win and how many he can afford to lose, but it is *how* he goes about trying to win those games that ultimately determines how many matches he will win or lose.

So, let's say that my objective at the start of the season is to win the league. I know that I will need to fall somewhere in line with the table below in terms of goals scored, goals conceded and, ultimately, points.

THE LAST FIVE PREMIER LEAGUE WINNERS

Year	Team	Goals for	Goals against	Points
2013–14	**Manchester City**	102	37	86
2012–13	**Manchester United**	86	43	89
2011–12	**Manchester City**	93	29	89
2010–11	**Manchester United**	78	37	80
2009–10	**Chelsea**	103	32	86

From this list we can determine that, in order to mount a serious challenge to the Premier League title, a team will need to score an average of 90.5 goals and concede an average of 36 goals over the course of the season. In doing so, they will hit an average number of points that will put them in with a great chance of winning the league.

In order to achieve these figures, the manager sets out his chosen formation, which he will rarely deviate from in the league – changes in formation usually come in Europe – and the personnel required to work best in the strategy that the manager has chosen to adopt. It may sound ridiculous, but it isn't when you consider how a manager sets his team up. It's all about balance. Quite simply, you can go down the

Liverpool or Manchester United route of two strikers (one dropping deep), who will score 20 to 25 goals each – or the Chelsea approach, which revolves around a solitary striker tasked with scoring at least 25 goals and a host of number 10s scoring 10 to 15 goals each. With well-rehearsed set pieces, coupled with centre-halves who attack everything coming into the box (John Terry and Gary Cahill), the team might add another 10 goals in the course of a season. Penalties, direct free-kicks and own goals can also nudge double figures in the course of a season.

THE ANOMALY THAT IS 'THE OPPOSITION'

The complexity of modern football is evident in every match. The ability of a team to deliver results isn't simply a case of how athletic they are or how technical they are, it depends more and more on their ability to absorb instructions from what are often mundane sessions out on the training pitch.

Managers always want to play the same players in the same formation. But sometimes a team will rock up and play with such determination and spirit that changes to the status quo are required in order to break the opposition down.

In January 2014 Chelsea visited Hull at the KC Stadium. At the time Hull were holding their own in the Premier League and were proving tough to beat – Manchester United had narrowly won there a few weeks earlier, 3–2, after going two goals down, and shortly after that the Tigers had walloped Fulham 6–0. As a side note, I did a column for Match of the Day 2 at Christmas in which I called Fulham 'a very ordinary team', something I took untold amounts of stick for, but I'm telling you that they were. But I digress.

During the match Hull were pinned back by Chelsea in what was perhaps the first instance of a Barcelona-style attacking philosophy being deployed in the Premier League. José Mourinho picked a team to put the maximum amount of pressure on Hull by occupying their back four at all times. He did this by playing a fluid, interchangeable formation of 3–3–4.

What made it work was the way the formation was executed. It didn't matter which players made up the four at the top of the pitch, just so long as there were always four players sitting on the toes and moving in between the Hull defenders. At one point the front four comprised Ashley Cole, Fernando Torres, David Luiz and César Azpilicueta – two full-backs and a centre-half, although, in truth, David Luiz was playing as a midfielder for almost the entire game. On another occasion John Terry made up one of the four before Mourinho shot up out of the dugout and told him to get back.

Playing in this very fluid way resulted in two things. Firstly, it restricted the opposition from passing out from the back, so nearly every ball the keeper – or any member of the back four – received was hit long. And Mourinho knew Hull would be playing with only one striker against two world-class centre-halves. No contest. Even if the striker took the ball down, where was he going to go? Hull could not get out of their half – Chelsea had so many men forward Hull literally did not have a pass on, there was no space for them to get the ball into the man who made their team tick, namely Tom Huddlestone.

Secondly, in a conventional football match, the midfielders know that they will be playing against other midfielders, the defenders know that they will be playing against one or possibly two strikers, and so on. In this match, Hull's entire team had no idea who they were supposed to be picking up, which players they were supposed to be tracking. If I were Tom Huddlestone, or his midfield partner Jake Livermore, I might expect to be playing against David Luiz or Ramires, and possibly a deep-lying striker in Eden Hazard. In reality, they played against a different three with almost every Chelsea attack and had no idea who they should be marking or when players would swap with the next three – and the same for went for Hull's back four: one minute their right-back would be up against Willian, the next he had to contend with Oscar or Ashley Cole.

It was fantastic to watch and, as a fan, you can get so much more enjoyment from a game of football – in particular, the games where you are neutral – if you are able to pick up on what is happening tactically. I find it enjoyable to see which player switches off first because, with so much movement and skill to contend with, it is only a matter of time before an inevitable slip-up.

So if this style of play is so effective, why don't all teams play like this? Well, ultimately, it's because they aren't good enough. But why? To find out, it's perhaps easier to study why the Chelsea players can do it.

It is important to realise that the level of concentration required to carry out tactics such as these is extremely high – especially when you could have been playing a different way the previous week, and will no doubt be playing yet

10 The ten greatest teams of all time

Barcelona, 2008–2012
Real Madrid, 1956–1960
Brazil, 1970
Ajax, 1971–1973
AC Milan, 1989–1994
Liverpool, 1977–1981
Manchester United, 1999
Real Madrid, 2002
Brazil, 2002
Ajax, 1995

another way a week later. That means José Mourinho has, at best, a week – well, four days with the Wednesday off, less with a mid-week game – to instil this week's tactics into his players. That is a feat in itself. It is even more impressive that the players can absorb these changing tactics and carry them out with such diligence.

On the pitch the game is moving so fast that sometimes you can get tunnel vision. The game appears slower from the stands, where spectators can see the entire pitch and all the bits of greenery in between the players, but down at eye level, all you see is twenty-odd players moving about extremely quickly, and you're having to manipulate a ball under pressure while performing a million calculations in your head about what you're going to do with the ball, where you're going to run, what the player in front of you might do, what the player behind him is going to do, where your striker is about to run, whether the ball is in a position where you can play it first time – and what the plan B is if the striker doesn't run and the ball isn't in the right place. It's almost too much at times, and all the while there are 50,000 fans telling you what you should be doing.

Now multiply all that by eleven: that is what the Chelsea players had to do. They had to be able to recognise that when one player came out of the four, another had to go in. Believe me, it was highly impressive stuff. Now imagine being a Barcelona player, and being able to do that frequently to the best players and teams in the world. That is how good those players are. The next time somebody tells you Barcelona are boring, tell them that they just don't understand what they're watching.

WHAT DOES ENGLAND NEED TO LEARN FROM ALL THIS?

I'm not sure if the England team are boring. I just feel that they are tactically in the Dark Ages. Take the game against San Marino at Wembley in 2012, for example. This was a World Cup qualifier and, although England were obviously never in any danger, it spoke volumes for the approach to tactics when Englishmen are left to their own devices.

England started the game with a conventional back four and two holding midfielders, and it took them thirty-five minutes to score – and even then the goal came from the penalty spot. They laboured to a 5–0 victory. Even at the time I remember being bemused but now, when I look back on that game, I simply marvel at the stupidity and ignorance of it. What, exactly, were England's players defending?

It is beyond logic that England needed to play with any centre-halves. San Marino never had any intention of leaving their own half and, even if they had, they weren't good enough to – they weren't quick enough to get away or skilful enough to manipulate the ball into areas that would ever hurt a top international team. José Mourinho would have realised this. He first tried his rotating four against Barcelona but, unfortunately, at a time when Barcelona were the greatest club side ever assembled, and they managed to outmanoeuvre even José's best efforts.

When Barcelona are faced with an opposition employing similar tactics to San Marino, they tend to play at least one midfielder as one of their two 'centre-halves'. As we've seen, they started this trend when they signed the Argentinian Javier Mascherano from Liverpool in 2010 and they continue to employ this method today – over the last couple of seasons they have played recognised midfielders such as Alex Song as a ball-carrying centre-half, as well as their preferred choice, Sergio Busquets, who is probably the most comfortable player you'll ever see on the ball. Barcelona have recognised that a ball-playing midfielder is a more effective centre-half than a John Terry-style centre-half given they rarely encounter an attacking threat that warrants a traditional back four. To put it another way, if a team has an average of 70 per cent possession in every game it plays, as well as averaging three goals per game, then why play a traditional back four? Well, the answer is simple: they don't, and that's why those figures are what they are.

So what have England learned from the greatest side ever assembled in world football, a side that continues to innovate and, in doing so, dictate the way football is played on the biggest stage?

Nothing.

The San Marino game was the perfect opportunity to play one if not two ball-playing midfielders as centre-halves. If they'd been available, Gerrard and Lampard could have played there without flinching. They have the range of passing and the knowledge of how to re-start attacks – plus, and this is the most important part, because it's where modern football is going: they are interchangeable. They are interchangeable with the players in front of them, such as Michael Carrick, Jack Wilshere, Tom Cleverley or Phil Jones, even Wayne Rooney. But Roy Hodgson didn't see it – or, rather, he bottled it.

Let me justify what I'm saying. The difference between players on the same team is that they specialise in one position and come to the fore when that speciality is tested – such as the job that Ashley Cole has done on Ronaldo countless times in the past. But Frank Lampard or Steven Gerrard would struggle against Ronaldo. Against a team with a limited threat, however, it becomes pointless to employ the type of specialised player in a role in which they're speciality isn't needed; in short, why play specialised players in a game where there is nothing to specialise against?

Years ago Barcelona and, as a result, Spain would come to realise this. Both teams started out by playing their full-backs as wingers and crowding the middle of the pitch with three or, at times, four incredibly talented midfielders who could all keep the ball and create chances. They learned that the best form of defence was ensuring the other team rarely had the ball. Later, they would move Lionel Messi in from the wing entirely and play him in the spaces left derelict by opposition players pulled out of position by the influx of midfielders. It didn't matter where in the last third of the pitch that space was, so long as Messi occupied it. Eventually, it was this realisation that hastened the demise of the traditional and, up to that point, extremely effective Barcelona 'front three'. The club has never stood still, it continues to evolve when seemingly at the sum of its powers.

It stands to reason that the more players there are who can keep the ball in advanced positions, the greater a team's chances of creating scoring opportunities. It starts with ball control. The better players do this by using one touch to bring the ball into their possession and at the same time placing it where it needs to be for the next pass. Too often I've see our youth team players take one touch to control the ball, another touch to control it again after the first one fails, then another to move the ball into a space a foot either side of them so they can (finally) make a pass. The problem is that if you need three touches to control a ball – and there are thousands who do – and set yourself for the next pass, then you will be closed down before you can get the pass away. What happens? The player ends up passing the ball backwards. This explains the value of the pressing game. If you don't have the ball then you can't pass it up the pitch towards the opposition goal; but if you press the opposition, then you can get them to do it for you. Barcelona, by passing and moving and controlling the ball with one touch instead of the two, are able to dominate teams and, most importantly, tire them out. In their opening game of the 2014–15 season at Camp Nou, opponents Elche played with eleven men behind the ball, yet even so, Barcelona hit the crossbar twice and, despite taking forty-two minutes to score their first goal, won at a canter 3–0. Amazingly, Barcelona also had their centre-half, Javier Mascherano, sent off almost immediately afterwards. Barcelona finished the match, having played for over half the game with only ten men, with 72 per cent of the possession, while Elche had no shots on target in the entire ninety minutes.

Perhaps the most interesting thing about Barcelona, though, is that their attacking philosophy does without a recognised striker. Instead, the club believe in having players who are comfortable in every area of the game. Take Andrés Iniesta, for example. I wouldn't call Iniesta a dribbler, or a holding midfielder, or a striker, or a box-to-box player – and yet he does every one of those things as well as any player in the world. In short, you don't need the best players in each position – you need the best players who know how to play as a team in the way the club and the manager wants them to play. Not every club can do that, of course, and there are smaller clubs that will succeed relative to their level by employing the absolute reverse of what I've said. But I'm talking about creating a dynasty and winning things at the very highest level – that's what excites me, not, I'm almost ashamed to say, launching the ball to a tall number 9 and winning the Conference league.

But there are English teams that are capable of putting these types of teams together, and there are managers in the Premier League who know only too well that the English are stuck in the Dark Ages. Arsène Wenger is a genius. When his club were at the top of the Premier League in January 2014, and the fans of the club and commentators far and wide were imploring him to sign another striker in case Olivier Giroud got injured, what did he do? He signed the midfielder Kim Källström, the type of player many thought would be the last on his list given that he had a clutch of attacking midfielders. That meant he wasn't stuck with a striker that he had overpaid for in a bubble market the following season, and that allowed him to sign the Barcelona striker, Alexis Sánchez. Think about it, the big picture is right in front of you.

Every time I speak to an Arsenal fan all I hear is that Wenger should sign this name and that name. So let me ask you a question. How many Arsenal fans would have signed the players that Wenger has signed over the years? Henry? Vieira? Ljungberg? None, because they would never have heard of them. How about Wilshere, Cazorla, Giroud, Gnabry or Koscielny? None, because nobody had ever heard of them either. That is true football knowledge – that is how to build a team, not a roster of names. And there is a massive, massive difference. I can recall hammering one of my former clubs to my agent after they signed an unknown player for £50,000. He went on to become a legend, achieving huge success with us and leaving for about £7 million. That was a lack of football knowledge on my part.

In England we are held back by ridiculous sayings, the worst of which is 'putting the ball in the net is the hardest thing in the game'. Let me tell you, right now, that is bullshit. Players from every position score every type of goal every Saturday of the season – but those chances are improved if the player is well-trained, educated in football, confident and doesn't panic. When the ball fell to Andrés Iniesta in the 2010 World Cup final, he didn't close his eyes and think, 'I hope this is on target.' He instinctively hit the ball across the goal and into the corner of the net because he'd been practising that technique every day since he was eight years old.

And there are examples of that kind of dedication to practice and repetitiveness everywhere we look in football. An old manager who I played under, a legend of the game and probably the most inspirational man I have ever worked with, used to preach the philosophy that a team should 'never, ever lose the ball in your own half'. Regaining possession in the opposition half accounts for around 40 per cent of goals scored from open play. And these 'regains' come from two main sources: players caught in possession; and what are known as 'in-balls'. In-balls are passes that are played infield by a full-back to a centre-midfielder that are cut out by an opposition player. If you watch the football highlights on any given weekend then I can guarantee that you'll see an in-ball that has been intercepted which results in a shot on goal.

An ever-decreasing number of goals are coming from crosses, and that has seen the trading in of the battering-ram number 9 for the introduction of the false number 9. Tactically, this has had a huge impact on the game. The full-back no longer plays the ball into the pitch, where teams are very often playing with three midfielders; instead, full-backs are starting higher up and carrying the ball forward, creating space for wide men to float inside into awkward positions. The result is that in-balls have been cut out and crosses are becoming rare.

In the 2013–14 season, Liverpool produced the lowest number of crosses in the Premier League, yet they finished second to Manchester City by just two points. Brendan Rodgers' team crossed the ball just over 400 times –

contrast that with Manchester United's near 800 crosses, as they endured their worst season since the Premier League began in 1992. Unsurprisingly, two-thirds of those crosses failed to find a teammate. Crossing is now seen as a weakness – an easy way to give the ball back to the opposition and a dangerous way to play given that one header out by a defender, or one clean catch by the goalkeeper, and suddenly the whole team is vulnerable to the counterattack. But how did football get to this point?

FASHION IN FOOTBALL

It may sound ridiculous but football goes through 'fashion' changes just like the high street – the main difference is, it happens over two or three years. Just after I started playing, it was very trendy to have a black, French holding midfielder in your team. That was largely the fault of Claude Makélélé, who was so outstanding in the position just in front of the back four that every manager up and down the Premier League tried to replicate it. But apart from the very best managers, most of them didn't appreciate Makélélé's most underrated and hidden talent.

During a team talk about Chelsea, ahead of a Premier League match at Stamford Bridge, our manager had decided that we would allow Makélélé to have the ball when we were defending. That meant that the rest of Chelsea's attacking unit would effectively be man-marked. At the time, Claude Makélélé was seen as the player who broke up opposition attacks – he tackled, tracked back, blocked and headed anything that might cause his team a threat. And that was largely how he was perceived by everyone outside of Chelsea; even Real Madrid did not see his greatness, selling him as they did to the Blues for £16.8 million, a relative bargain given the size and financial power of the two clubs involved. The Frenchman would go on to become so integral for Chelsea that he even spawned a name for his own position – 'the Makélélé role'. OK, not the most imaginative title ever, but then football tends to call a spade a spade. I give you 'the Cruyff turn'.

Unfortunately, where our tactics were concerned, we had fallen for the general perception of Claude Makélélé rather than the reality. It was easy to do – unless you were a top coach or scout, you'd never have spotted it. Clearly, somebody at Chelsea had. When the game kicked off, we retreated and allowed Makélélé to have the ball. Claude Makélélé scored two goals for Chelsea in 144 games; in our game he could have had a hat trick but for some last-ditch tackling and the frame of the goal. He ran the show from start to finish, he carried the ball forward and passed with aplomb and, in the process, he taught me a valuable lesson. All of the top players are capable of filling in and assuming the role of others, they have a general level of footballing ability and awareness that is beyond most other players at inferior teams playing in their specialised positions.

Our assessment of Makélélé and, by extension, the match was flawed from the start due to a fundamental breakdown in the basics of football analytics. In this case we had overlooked the fact that Makélélé was a world-class professional footballer. I know that sounds ridiculous but it is a reminder, if one were needed, that even Premier League teams are occasionally swept up in the basic popular perception of what a certain footballer brings to the party.

The truth is that Claude Makélélé was integral to Chelsea's success for another reason. The cause behind his style was to break up the play, and that was the tag the pundits, the public and even other teams felt comfortable branding him with. The net result was that he was Chelsea's most effective attacking player. During his time with the team, nobody started more Chelsea attacks than Claude Makélélé. It stands to reason that if a player breaks the play up then the responsibility will ultimately fall to that same player to play the first pass out, and Makélélé was an underrated expert in that field. Given the time that we gave him on the ball he duly ripped us to pieces.

Today there are many players who feel the job of dismantling the play stops the moment the ball is won, and that a pass back to the goalkeeper is a job well done. That thinking is flawed. The moment the ball is travelling to the goalkeeper, the game becomes one of chance. The ball will invariably be kicked forward, because if you're breaking the play up then you're doing so in your own half, and if a team has committed men forward then you will not have time to play it out to the full-backs. So with the ball in the air one of two things will happen: it will either be flicked on to nobody because there is a lone striker up front, or the team will head it back into a minefield where anything can happen because the defending team hasn't been able to regroup.

Makélélé had very quick feet – he could turn very quickly thanks to a low centre of gravity, and he was deceptively speedy over the first five yards. In fact, even when he got up a head of speed, he took some stopping. But it was his passing that did the damage: he always played the right pass at the right time, and that is down to awareness. He knew when a team had overcommitted – so he would turn and play out to a wide man or play a through-ball – and he knew when to play it safe by looking for a full-back. That is an instinctive knowledge of the game, which comes from playing firstly with the brain and then with the eyes: if you know roughly what the shape of a team will be at any given moment, even when your back is to the play, then you have a great advantage when it comes to decision-making on the ball. If you can pre-empt what those around you may do then the game becomes so much easier, and it is surprisingly easy to do – it's simply a matter of trusting your own judgement.

YOU WILL BENEFIT AS A PLAYER SO LONG AS YOU KNOW WHERE TO LOOK AND UNDERSTAND WHAT IS REALLY HAPPENING AROUND YOU

In May 2014, after becoming chairman of the FA, Greg Dyke, a man with very limited football background, set out the recommendations proposed by what some believe to be a rather questionable committee that he had installed a year earlier. Dyke had started from the premise that England would reach the semi-finals of Euro 2020 and win the World Cup in 2022 – a very popular mandate that probably went some way to getting him the job. To reach the semi-finals he'd need to solve the problem of why there weren't more kids coming through our academies who were going on to become England internationals. Dyke reasoned that if the pool of players was bigger, and the players had more opportunity to play, then they would ultimately benefit the England team for many years to come.

What came back was a wretched proposal for a newly formed League Three that would sit in between League Two and the Conference, populated by Premier League B teams. Dyke's plan was to let the country's most talented kids travel around England, playing on terrible pitches against men who would try to hurt them because of their Premier League connections, and against systems and formations that largely bypass the essence of top-level football. So Dyke's plan to give these kids more game time in order to be better prepared for a future with the England team was to expose them to the worst traits within the British game by placing them at a level that would be detrimental to their international prospects.

But even throwing these kids into an environment where the good things they may have learned would be rendered useless is eclipsed by the fact that the coaching in this country is fundamentally flawed. A few years ago the FA decided that the reason most of our talent wasn't good enough to progress was that there weren't enough coaches at grass-roots level. So they embarked on a ridiculous crusade to train more coaches. Now, you don't need me to tell you that having more of something is no guarantee that the product will become better. Apple won't produce better computers by ramming their factories with more staff on the conveyor belt; they'll simply continue to produce more computers of the same standard.

While the drive to train more coaches was going on, the FA were paying for a stadium that had run way over budget.

Initially, the cost of building a state-of-the-art Wembley was set at £445 million – the final figure came in at £962 million. And, although the FA did well to secure a fixed-cost contract, the developers, Multiplex, kicked up such a fuss over the job being not quite as it was sold to them that work was held up and the FA had to step in to negotiate an agreement on compensation and liability. Staring down the barrel of a shortfall, the FA had to generate extra income and set the wheels in motion to bid for the 2018 World Cup, having (perhaps luckily due to construction delays) missed out on hosting the 2006 World Cup to Germany. But its other plans to raise money were not as dependent on a third-party decision as the World Cup is with FIFA, and the drive to produce more coaches went ahead.

David Sheepshanks, the St George's Park National Football Centre chairman, was tasked with spinning the positive PR around the plans, and he did so by highlighting the chronic lack of grass-roots coaches. In 2012 he said, 'As things stand, Spain have 25,000 UEFA A, B and pro-licence coaches, Italy 30,000, Germany 35,000 while England have 6000.' To all intents and purposes it appeared as if the FA had identified a legitimate weakness in the coaching of the players in England, and from that point the FA would drive the expansion of a coaching programme that would attempt to match, if not better, the number of coaches found on the Continent.

What David Sheepshanks and the FA omitted from their mandate was the cost to those who wanted to obtain a UEFA A coaching licence. In Germany it costs £985 to complete the course, in Spain the price is £435. In England the same licence costs between £2500 and £3500. It is one example of a whole range of money-generating schemes put in place to pay down debt incurred by Wembley. Often, such schemes are hastily put together with a thin layer of PR wrapped around them, usually with a 'national interest' twang added, and nearly always these schemes are doomed to failure because they are undermined by a lack of basic due diligence from the start as well as other, more pressing, motives that need to be served. In short, you can stump up the cash for your coaching badges but you'd better make sure that you have a friend on the inside, because nobody cares about your little badge in the game. It's a closed shop, and the FA only care that you've paid in full.

So how does all that tie in with coaching today? In this country coaching is a 'jobs for the boys' culture. That is to say, if you played with somebody who is now a manager, then there is every chance that you will fit into his set-up somewhere along the line and, often, old mates end up as the youth team coach or running the academy. In this country, any coach who is involved in the youth team set-up is there because he isn't good enough to coach the first team yet – he's cutting his teeth, as they say, learning his trade.

Hundreds of years ago I played against Adi Viveash, a centre-half who wore a mouthguard. Today he is the Chelsea youth team manager, and in 2013–14 I watched as his side beat Fulham over two legs to win the FA Youth Cup. It was, quite frankly, extremely depressing. Chelsea played with one up front and were desperate not to lose. For me, as a footballer who knows his apples, on the outside looking in at Chelsea, it was nothing more than Adi Viveash replicating José Mourinho, because he knows that if all the stars line up one day and he has achieved the bare minimum that is expected of a Chelsea youth team manager, then he might, just possibly, get the top job.

Now, liken that approach to that of a friend of mine who works as a youth team coach for Anderlecht. 'We want our players to be fluid,' he told me. 'We don't want them to feel stuck in one position and rely on other teammates to help them out. What we do is expose them to the dangers that other teams can offer, because that is how they will improve. We don't want to play with four players across our defence, we want to play with three so that our players become better one-against-one defenders. We want our midfielders and attacking players to interchange and take up positions where they can hurt teams, not the positions where the opposition know where to find them. We want wingers to come inside and centre midfielders to overlap. When Vincent Kompany was here, we coached him how to play as a midfielder so that he was comfortable on the ball. Now he plays at centre-half for one of the biggest teams in the world, and you can see that when he has the ball he can dribble, turn, step-over and pass. He is a complete player.'

In England we have a history of putting square pegs in round holes: while Anderlecht were training their players, including Kompany, to be comfortable on the ball so that they would make better defenders, Tottenham were trying to turn their best centre-half, Ledley King, into a midfielder, years after his formative coaching had dictated that he'd never be able to play in that position. Eventually the club fell into the same Makélélé trap as everybody else and signed the Ivory Coast international, Didier Zokora, in 2006.

But English football has been misreading the tectonic tactical plates for years. When West Ham signed the Argentinian international Javier Mascherano from Corinthians, they thought they were signing one of the most highly rated midfield players in the world, but the financial deal around him meant that West Ham never realised his potential because it was in the interests of the third-party owner that he move on again quickly and earn them a huge commission. Those problems eventually saw Mascherano move to Liverpool, where he went on to play as a centre-midfielder for three years. When I played against Mascherano he was just another holding midfield player that our team had to navigate around. At the time Liverpool were relying on Fernando Torres for goals, with Steven Gerrard supporting him and Xabi Alonso supporting both with the initial pass.

When Liverpool lost the ball, Mascherano would go haring towards it and, so long as you could bypass him, you were at Liverpool's back four. We dominated the match we played against Liverpool at home by moving Mascherano all around the pitch like a moth to the flame – in football we call it 'dragging him around', and managers utilise the tactic when they want somebody out of the way. We achieved it by sending one of our strikers into a wide position as a decoy and, sure enough, Mascherano followed – and once he'd left his hole we sent a midfielder through the middle and pushed the opposite wide man and full-back high up the pitch. Liverpool couldn't cope. From then on, other teams copied us and achieved results. What our scouts had cleverly worked out was that there was more to be gained by isolating a weakness than there was in identifying Liverpool's danger men; we had realised that Liverpool had an Achilles heel that would undermine their entire playing strategy – in short, remove Mascherano from his zone, and you would also remove every threat that Liverpool had.

But while we patted each other on the back within the confines of our changing rooms, and the players had their usual say on the opposition – 'that Mascherano is basic' – somebody else was appraising the Argentinian's performance: a club, actually, and they were based in Spain. They were called Barcelona, and they were about to produce the finest club side of all time.

When Javier Mascherano signed for the Catalan giants for €24 million (euros) most of us scratched our heads. There was no way he was good enough to play for a club that big, there must have been a mistake, some kind of shady deal, a way of moving money around before he went to whichever club his agents were trying to get him to. But there he stayed and, even more bizarrely, he played, and not in midfield either, but at centre-half. Here was a player who, only a couple of years earlier, had been exposed by my club as a possible weak link, playing for one of the biggest clubs in world football. And they were playing him at centre-half. So far during his time as centre-half for Barcelona Mascherano has won the domestic title twice, the Champions League, the Copa del Rey, the Supercopa de España twice, the UEFA Super Cup and the FIFA Club World Cup, as well as becoming a World Cup finalist in 2014.

All that was made possible because Barcelona had discovered that, in a team that kept the ball, a player such as Mascherano was the perfect cover at centre-half. He was comfortable on the ball, he was strong, he was quick across the ground and he was brave. Pep Guardiola, the Barcelona manager, had come to realise that Claude Makélélé started Chelsea's attacks and his rationale told him that if he took that player out and put him at centre-half then he could not only start attacks directly from the back four, he would also have one extra attacking player. And it all rested on finding a midfielder who could play at centre-half.

But it wasn't just Barcelona who had worked out why Makélélé was so valuable to the Chelsea team. In August 2009 the Blues signed a young Serbian player called Nemanja Matić. He was an attacking midfielder of a good standard, but he wasn't at the level needed to displace Chelsea's other attacking midfield stars and, in 2011, he was used as a makeweight in a deal that saw Benfica centre-half David Luiz move to Stamford Bridge for £21 million.

At Benfica, under the guidance of manager Jorge Jesus, Matić was converted from a playmaker to a defensive midfielder and became the star of a Benfica team that won the Taça de Liga Cup, finished as runners-up in the Portuguese Primeira Liga and runners-up to Chelsea in the Europa League final. On a personal note Matić was named second place in the FIFA Puskás Award. Despite the hat trick of runners-up places, or maybe because of them, Chelsea parted with £21 million in January 2014 to re-sign a player they'd originally bought for £1.5 million seven years earlier.

There is nothing accidental about good coaching. In fact, there is nothing accidental about the lack of quality coaching in this country at youth team level. Very often youth team coaches are instructed to play as the first team do and, to anybody reading this, it probably makes sense.

But such thinking is fundamentally flawed. The object of our academies and youth team set-ups is to produce players for the first team or, at the very least, players of value who can be sold to smaller teams. To do that they have to be trained to be technically brilliant and match-ready; they have to be trained to be comfortable on the ball and make the right decisions. As it currently stands, our youth teams are being trained to win at all costs, which sounds good but does nothing to benefit their technical ability, because any team can defend for ninety minutes without really touching the ball before scoring from a set piece.

I based the opinions I have about grass-roots football not on guesswork and hearsay but on what I've seen with my own eyes. In my second book, *Tales from the Secret Footballer*, I told a story of my son's first football match, in which he was thrown in at the deep end about a week after he joined his new teammates. The reason was simple: I knew it, the manager knew it and I suspect even some of the parents knew it. He is left-footed and because of that he and other kids like him will always be banished to the left-back or left-wing position. Even Gareth Barry was thrown into the left-back position and wasn't switched to midfield until he was a first-team player.

During that game, the kids were encouraged to 'get rid of it', 'put it out' and 'tackle', by both the management teams and the parents standing alongside the pitch, who are supposed to remain silent throughout. My son's team won the match for no other reason than that they had the biggest players. In fact, it seemed to me that the whole team were on the taller side of their age group, which has since made me think about something that Dutch midfielder Ronald de Boer, legendary Ajax player and now assistant manager, once said: 'When I see English boys playing – at twelve, thirteen, fourteen years old – I always have the feeling they put winning first. No, it should be developing first. When you have a big guy who is twelve but looks like a fourteen- or fifteen-year-old boy, of course he wins against the guy who is small. But the guy who is small is learning how to kick a ball, what's around him – and that's what we focus on. It's not the end result that you win, it's at the end he's going to be a great player.'

Unfortunately, even our top academies have decided to focus on playing to win. This is bad news for the game: if we have a group of coaches within our academies whose success is based primarily on winning cups and titles rather than bringing through individual players on their own merits – which is how success should be measured – then the numbers of players coming through and their quality will remain where it has been for twenty-five years. The FA knows that it cannot break that stranglehold: it cannot force clubs to employ better coaches, and it cannot back another drive for more coaches so quickly after the last one because people will begin asking awkward questions. It is no surprise to me that we have a lack of talent that goes on to play at international level.

There is no doubt that the Premier League brand has become far more valuable by opening up its doors to foreign players, which in turn has opened up the doors to foreign TV markets. The more cosmopolitan the league, the more markets are interested in licensing the product. Remember that phase a few years back when players from the Far East began arriving on these shores? It wasn't by accident. The trend is said to have started with Manchester City and Sun Jihai, a Chinese player who enjoyed a good career with City from 2002, before moving to Sheffield United and then back to China. Manchester United promptly followed suit with the arrival of Park Ji-sung, the South Korean player. At that time Manchester United were exploding with commercial potential and the Far East was an untapped and extremely lucrative proposition. In 2002 the World Cup had been staged jointly in South Korea and Japan and Park had been exceptional, scoring three goals during a run to the semi-finals. In July 2005 United paid Dutch club PSV Eindhoven £4 million for Park's services.

For the first time, global commercial opportunity was affecting the players teams bought, depending on where they were from and which markets were booming. In July of 2006 Reading FC purchased another South Korean winger, Seol Ki-hyeon, from English side Wolverhampton Wanderers. Reading were newly promoted to the Premier League and were looking to capitalise on the boom in the Far East. Seol Ki-hyeon's arrival saw the club invited to play in the Peace Cup, a pre-season tournament held in South Korea. The arrival of Seol at Reading came after a sponsorship deal had been struck between Reading FC and multinational electronics and ceramics manufacturer, Kyocera, based in Kyoto, Japan. The global market was now available to all.

And that meant that the first team that could truly capture the imagination of a worldwide audience stood to gain financially, by levels never seen before.

TAKING ADVANTAGE OF THE GLOBAL AUDIENCE

In 1988 Barcelona appointed the legendary player Johan Cruyff as their new manager. Immediately, the triple Ballon d'Or winner, nurtured under the famed Dutch coaching philosophy of 'total football' (where players were taught to play in almost any position), set about imposing a style of play on his side that, eighteen years later, would come to be known, at the same club, by the term 'tiki-taka'. Cruyff coupled his single-minded vision with his own training as a player and led Barcelona to the first European Cup triumph in the club's history, beating a star-studded Sampdoria 1–0 at Wembley in 1992. In 1994 they would make the final again and, although soundly beaten by an AC Milan side many still argue was the most talented club side ever assembled, it was clear to all that Cruyff was on to something.

When Cruyff left his role as manager in 1996, the long-term effects of his football ideals were still, largely, to show their hand. Publicly, he had taken the team to new heights but, privately, he had revolutionised the club's youth policy. When Cruyff became the manager of Barcelona he presented a vision to José Luís Núñez, the club's newly elected president. That vision included an updated model of the original Ajax philosophy of coaching players to avoid tackling and the physicality of the game, to play to their strengths in retaining possession and passing around their opponents with a series of short, sharp passes. This was tiki-taka.

The evolution of football doesn't just happen – nearly every player I know who went on to become a manager learned most, if not all, of their footballing beliefs through the one style of play that more than likely brought them their biggest success as a player. The mark of a great manager depends on whether he can evolve the style he has chosen. La Masia – the academy that would be tasked with producing the players with Barcelona's philosophy ingrained in them – began paying dividends almost immediately and, two years after Cruyff had laid down the template, the first trainee who would go on to play regularly for the club came through the system – his name was Pep Guardiola.

Managers came and went but La Masia remained a constant. Frank Rijkaard, another Dutch legend coached by Ajax, embraced La Masia and led the team to another European Cup triumph, two Supercopas de España and two La Liga titles before, eventually, Pep Guardiola took over the reins. With a team that on occasion was made up entirely of players from the La Masia academy, Guardiola embarked on a period of success with Barcelona that would include three La Liga titles, two Copa del Rey victories, three Supercopas de España, two Champions League successes, two UEFA Super Cups and two FIFA Club World Cups. During one season, they won every title the club had entered and had to have a debate about which competition badge should appear on the players' shirts the following season.

Importantly, the club went with Guardiola. They set out a vision to achieve a further million paying members in four years, they took shirt sponsorship for the first time in the club's history and, recently, the Catalan club announced a £500 million redevelopment of a stadium that will seat 105,000 fans, after which it will sell the naming rights. Barcelona, this fiercely independent Catalan club, had to engage with the modern global marketplace because of the success of a group of players and a manager who mostly grew up not 20 miles from the stadium itself.

And those players included two of the greatest midfield players of all time: Xavi Hernández and Andrés Iniesta. No matter what angle a player approached either of these players they always seemed to be able to turn away from danger. My friend can explain better than I can; he played against them for Chelsea in the Champions League: 'Whenever I thought I had Xavi cornered, he'd turn away from me. The faster I closed him down, the easier it was for him to escape me. He has a sixth sense, an understanding not only of where he is in space but of where everybody else is. I don't know how he does it but I wish I knew.'

Xavi and Iniesta aren't pulling a fast one, they aren't performing something that can't be replicated, they are simply displaying sleight of mind. And it can be learned because largely it comes from your own experiences on the football pitch – it is simply a question of how deep you are willing to go into this game of ours. If you are willing to learn and remember simple things that helped you out of a situation, then you will be the better for it. Some players re-watch something they did in a match and marvel at themselves; others watch the same thing and remember how they did it. Not only that, they intuitively understand how it happened, where the other players were, what made it possible and where else on the pitch it might work.

It's like starting out with a jigsaw at the age of five and gradually putting the pieces in place over a thirty-year period. Some people will do it as the experiences happen to them, and some will need to see the same piece ten or twenty times before working out where it fits. What made Xavi and Iniesta so good at this was the coaching they had in their formative years.

IT'S ALL CLAUDE MAKÉLÉLÉ'S FAULT

Unfortunately, peaks in football never last. Eventually somebody would come up with an answer to tiki-taka that, depending on how you like watching football, would push the sport towards a less pretty, more sedate and, ultimately, chess-like game for large periods. While Bayern Munich and Dortmund would eventually fight fire with fire with a brand of football as exciting as that, we first had to undergo the painful process of watching supposedly great managers try to stifle Barcelona's game.

When José Mourinho became manager of Real Madrid he had to break the Barcelona stranglehold. He tried almost everything: he kicked Barcelona and, in particular, Lionel Messi, to bits; he tried to go after them higher up the pitch – but Barcelona were so good they simply played around Madrid, the culmination of which was a 5–0 drubbing at the Nou Camp. In that game there was an example of how brilliantly simple tiki-taka can be and why it works so well provided it is done quickly and with precision.

It happened for the first goal. Arguably, to this day, outside of the top clubs, teams refuse to push sides back by passing up the pitch. Certainly the lower down the divisions you go, the more likely it is that teams gain ground by playing down the channels and looking for crosses or throw-ins and corners. In the first goal Messi passed forward to Iniesta, who stopped the ball for him

Barcelona v Real Madrid

Direction of Barcelona attack ▶

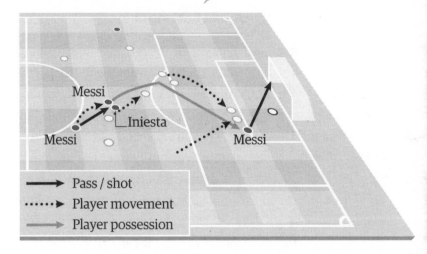

to run on to before moving off again. It was that simple – a little thing that makes such a huge difference to what the opposition do, and the shape of the game as a result. I first saw the American player Claudio Reyna do it against my team for Manchester City and, at first, I couldn't work out how City were getting up the pitch so easily. I studied that game for a long time, looking for some complicated football algorithm, where, in reality, it was extremely basic.

When Reyna got the ball, he would push it through to a deep-lying striker or an advanced midfielder in between the gap behind our midfielders and in front of our back four. The striker stopped it dead, moved away into another space, and Reyna stepped on to the ball. Now, what would happen to the two teams at the most fundamental level?

Well, Manchester City would collectively step up five yards, which squeezed the pitch, and our defence would instinctively drop off five yards. When you hear the commentator saying that a team cannot get out of their half, this is the reason it is happening. In one short pass Claudio Reyna was gaining his team a total of 10 extra yards to play with, 10 yards that were closer to our goal. In doing so, they had more men in better positions to be effective in the final third, and our team had fewer players capable of attacking them.

What tends to happen is that the opposition become scared of the striker or advanced midfielder in behind them so they drop off to stop the player receiving the ball, and suddenly players like Reyna have more freedom to work in – and with more freedom they can start to dictate the play. When this version is scaled up so that an entire team is able to play this way, including the centre-halves, and the other nine outfield players are all bursting their lungs to create a passing option then it becomes incredibly difficult to stop. The biggest problem in the style of play employed by many teams not at the top of the tree is that they don't play where the best space is, they play the ball to where the most space is.

But at the highest level football continually evolves, and in the 2012–13 Champions League semi-finals, the German clubs Bayern Munich and Borussia Dortmund both found the antidote. In truth, these clubs had been following Barcelona's La Masia academy for a decade, drawn to it by a German sense of efficiency and sustainability, but also lured by the reasoning that if Spanish kids could play that way, there was no reason why German kids couldn't.

Ten years later, Bayern and Dortmund took on the might of Spain with teams that relied heavily on home-grown players while blending their tactics with a mix of tiki-taka and, when they'd win the ball back from the team that was pressing them, blistering counterattacking football. And it worked. Bayern Munich destroyed Barcelona 7–0 over two legs, while Dortmund crushed Real Madrid 4–1 at home and, despite losing the second leg 2–0, they would make it through to the final to face their German counterparts in a match that would see Munich crowned as the masters of this new approach following a late 2–1 victory at Wembley.

As so often happens in football, the approach was mimicked. Real Madrid, who had not won the Champions League since 2002, reached the final in 2014 by taking the new German philosophy to the extreme. As we know, once Real Madrid decide how they are going to play, they buy the best players for the job – and so it proved again when, in the summer of 2013, they smashed the world transfer record to bring the best counterattacking player on the planet to the Bernabéu, for £85.3 million.

When I played against Gareth Bale he was a young professional still trying to find his way. He'd signed for Tottenham for a reported £8.5 million, as a left-back, and was given the 'unlucky' tag by pundits because every time he played for the team in his early days Tottenham failed to win. And then, one summer, the Tottenham fitness coaches noted that Bale was smashing the times set for sprint training and, in turn, they reported their findings to the coaching team. Bale had come through the Southampton youth set-up, an academy at the forefront of developing kids in England by teaching them to be comfortable on the ball as well as improving their speed and fitness, to make sure that the pick of the players were ready, almost immediately, to play first-team football. Eventually, Tottenham realised they'd actually bought a lightning-quick winger who was very competent with the ball at high speed, and they set about improving him further. Gareth Bale would go on to make his name during two Champions League performances against the Inter Milan full-back, Maicon, where his scintillating pace and eye for goal led to the Brazilian waiting by the tunnel to applaud the Welshman off the field. My friends were at both games and they told me that whenever Bale sped past Maicon, the Inter full-back would chase him until the move had finished, after which he'd shake his head with a wry smile. Nobody had ever seen anything like this before.

In Real Madrid's two semi-final matches against Bayern Munich they allowed the German champions to have possession of the ball, and when they won it back Cristiano Ronaldo, Karim Benzema and Ángel Di María would set off at pace with one target: to score a goal. In the second leg, away from home, manager Carlo Ancelotti added Gareth Bale to the line-up, and Munich simply couldn't live with him. Over those two matches Real Madrid managed to score against the European champions no fewer than five times, four of them away from home.

THE 2014 CHAMPIONS LEAGUE FINAL – THE CULMINATION

In the final Real Madrid came up against the masters of sitting in and defending, then exposing teams on the counterattack. Atlético Madrid also had a third, more staple dimension to their game: they were incredibly strong at set pieces, and the result was a first – a team that blended tiki-taka, counterattacking football, clever set pieces and resolute defending into a single strategy. Atlético Madrid had sat on top of La Liga going into the final day of the 2013–14 season ahead of a title-deciding match against Barcelona at the Nou Camp, a match in which every facet of their strategy was utilised. Atlético kept Barcelona out of their box for long stretches, and despite losing their talismanic striker Diego Costa and going a goal down they equalised through Diego Godín's powerful header from a 48th-minute corner. They held on to win their first La Liga title in eighteen years and break a duopoly on the crown that had been held by Barcelona and neighbours Real Madrid for almost a decade. When the final whistle sounded, 99,000 Barcelona fans stood as one and applauded them.

Pundits and managers alike lauded Atlétcio manager Diego Simeone for challenging the might of Barcelona and Real Madrid when many had seen it as an impossible task. It was made all the more impressive by the fact that in the close season he'd been forced to sell €70 million of talent. But Simeone had built his team from a single foundation, adding layers as he went. His initial goal hadn't been rocket science but was something that, given the game is a team sport, is incredibly difficult to achieve: getting the team to work harder than the opposition and, above all, work for each other.

It is a fundamental law of football. I have seen teams nowhere near as talented as their opposition achieve results because they are more committed. I've also played in teams with that mentality and achieved remarkable things as a result. I have also played in what is known in the game as 'a team of names' – seriously talented individuals who simply could not play together as a team.

In the 2014 Champions League final, Atlético came within two minutes of beating the mighty Real Madrid and, in truth, they should have won. They'd scored their goal through another Diego Godín header from a corner, living up to their reputation as the masters of set pieces, but then, ironically, conceded to a Sergio Ramos header in stoppage time from a Madrid corner. In extra-time Atlético simply ran out of energy and the counterattacking prowess of Madrid would do for them no fewer than three times, as Real finished up 4–1 winners.

Understanding the fashions and trends that football throws up is key for both managers and players. It ultimately helps managers to work out new formations in order to stay ahead of the curve or, indeed, those managers who are trying to catch up. As a player, it can help you to make the right move. Gareth Bale moved to Real Madrid for a number of factors, some of which were out of his hands, such as the transfer fee and the history of the club. But, ultimately, Bale knew that Madrid suited him perfectly – the club explained the tactical direction that it was heading in and that he would be a huge part of it. For once Madrid signed a player who would complement the team rather than a megastar who had been signed purely to appease the fans. Eighty-five million pounds seems expensive, but the premium comes from the fact that only one other player can do what Bale does, and with top clubs in modern football now digging in for long periods in matches, he can't do it on his own any more. His name is Cristiano Ronaldo, and he also plays for Real Madrid.

HOW DO YOU STOP A PLAYER LIKE CRISTIANO RONALDO?

The way managers ponder that question today is very often the reason that their tactics are flawed. The question is not how to stop an individual player; rather, how to stop the team. At the level Real Madrid operate at, stopping Ronaldo is only part of the battle. At the end of last season the Real Madrid attacker boasted a record of 177 goals in 166 games.

But it wasn't always like that. When Ronaldo played for Manchester United it was easier to stop him; when he began his career at Sporting Lisbon, and in his first couple of seasons with United, he was more of a clear-cut winger who roamed down the line. Eventually, he began cutting inside and thereafter he had earned a licence to go wherever he wanted so long as he kept his shape when the team defended. That was the moment when football really began to change, tactically. In my lifetime Ronaldo was the first player who pushed the concept of attacking with a completely open and fluid mind-set – instead of attacking

Most followed in world:
@cristiano
28.5 million

as a unit, within which one or two strikers had to make the box, one winger crossed the ball, the other winger made the back post, and an attacking midfielder tried to make a late run into the penalty area. Those starting positions still exist within the game, but they are fluid – if a striker like Wayne Rooney leaves the penalty area then his place can be taken by a narrow winger, while Rooney himself is comfortable enough on the ball to keep the move evolving.

Manchester United had exhausted the standard 4–4–2 model in the days of Giggs, Keane, Scholes and Beckham across the midfield, with Cole and Yorke up front. Most teams dug in and defended for their lives, but those forward-thinking managers – the managers who didn't want to play second fiddle and who saw United's dominance as a challenge to overcome – stepped up to the plate.

Arsène Wenger, the Arsenal manager installed in August 1996, was credited by many with producing the first 'moneyball'-type team within football. 'Moneyball' is the term given to a team made up of players with enormous potential based on their stats but who have been undervalued in the transfer market for a number of reasons. The man credited with popularising the strategy was the baseball coach, Billy Beane, who took the role of general manager with the unfashionable team, the Oakland A's. In 2002 the A's became the first team in over a hundred years of baseball to win twenty games in a row. In fact, Wenger pre-dated Beane's appointment at the A's by over a year.

In just his second season in charge of the Gunners Wenger won the league and Cup double, proving that his method of signing largely unknown players could work at the highest level. Players such as Patrick Vieira, a reserve player at AC Milan signed by Wenger for £3.5 million, and Emmanuel Petit from Marseille for £2.5 million – both of whom would go on to win the World Cup with France in 1998. Elsewhere, Marc Overmars, a speedy winger from Ajax, was signed for the relatively modest sum of £5 million and would go on to become the finest winger in Europe before both he and Petit were later sold to Barcelona for a combined fee of £32 million. And up front an unknown teenager, who went by the name of Nicolas Anelka, arrived from France with a reputation for blistering pace and an eye for goal – signed for a bargain £500,000 by Wenger, he would later be sold to Real Madrid for £23 million.

Wenger was building a team in a way that few people in the game had seen before. He did it initially by bringing in players he knew of, players he had perhaps worked with but who had now fallen into reserve sides at other clubs, like Patrick Vieira. But it is his scouting system that is most impressive. Wenger realised that it was far better to have multiple experts around the world who would agree on one player before sending their suggestion back to Arsenal's in-house scout, who in turn informed Wenger. Every football club plays at least once a week, so what was needed were more bodies on the ground. I was told that eighty Brazilian players of a similar age, playing in central midfield, were rejected before one found his way on to Wenger's DVD player. The one that got through, and was ultimately signed, was Denílson.

Through Wenger's philosophy, Arsenal challenged Manchester United for every trophy in the English game.

During that time Arsenal would wrest the Premier League crown away from their rivals in 2001–02 and 2003–04.

But Manchester United were the bigger club, the bigger brand, and already had the stadium in place to ensure match-day revenues were unlike anything any other team could match. But that didn't stop Alex Ferguson casting enviable glances towards Wenger's revolution in north London.

In 2001 Ferguson broke the British transfer record to sign Juan Sebastián Verón from Lazio, for £28.1 million, but unfortunately for United the game was already changing. Verón was labelled a flop: he didn't have the time on the ball that he'd enjoyed in Italy and, despite Ferguson's assertion to the media that 'Verón is a fucking great player and you're all fucking idiots', it was clear that he was not suited to Manchester United. Although Verón did manage to win the Premier League crown while at Old Trafford, in 2002–03, his contribution amounted to only two goals in 25 league games. He was sold to Chelsea the next season for a cut-price £15 million.

Ferguson had realised that the football landscape had shifted: pace was now the order of the day, Arsenal and Chelsea were challenging thanks to solid defences and lightning-fast wingers. Fortunately, he was holding all of the aces: United could afford to bring in the best talent (it just had to be suited to the style of the Premier League) and he could also afford to take punts on top young talent that could supplement the team. In 2003 he signed a youngster from Sporting Lisbon for €15 million called Cristiano Ronaldo.

It took a few seasons for the young Portuguese to harness his early promise, but in 2006–07 he broke through the twenty-goal barrier for the first time and, in doing so, helped United to reclaim the Premier League title after three barren years. But it was the style of the team that was benefiting Ronaldo. From 2006 Sir Alex Ferguson played a fluid front three of Wayne Rooney, Park Ji-sung and Cristiano Ronaldo; in 2007 Carlos Tevez came in for Park and the results were explosive.

Manchester United went on to claim a hat trick of titles, each more impressive than the last, with Ronaldo scoring 31 league goals in 34 games in 2007–08 and 18 in 33 in 2008–09. In his time at Old Trafford he won the PFA player of the year and young player of the year, along with the PFA fans' player of the year and the Football Writers' Association footballer of the year, becoming the first player to win all four awards.

Sir Alex Ferguson, driven by the competition around him, had radically altered United's style of play by attacking with three players who were supported by a strong midfield who, in turn, were supported by two advanced full-backs. The triple-head attack revolutionised football and, although Chelsea had had success by playing with a solitary striker in Didier Drogba, and United themselves had used Ruud van Nistelrooy as a solitary striker to great effect, this was the first time that a team had three distinctive, interchanging front men who could go where they pleased.

The fluidity of United's front three was best shown by two line-ups in the same season. In the 2007–08 season, United were drawn to play Roma in the first leg of the Champions League quarter-final. Ferguson picked a front three of Rooney on the left, Ronaldo through the middle and Park on the right. United reverted to a five when they lost the ball in deep areas and a three when they were higher up the pitch, with Paul Scholes squeezing in on Roma's first pass out. From the outset, Roma's game plan was clear: kick Ronaldo whenever he had the ball and try to intimidate him. It left an awful lot of other United players free to roam around.

Initially, however, the approach worked: Ronaldo became increasingly disillusioned with the game and the referee, who seemed to be siding with the home crowd in the opening exchanges. His patience could be seen to be wearing thin when, in the first half, he attempted a free-kick from fully 40 yards that just about made it off the pitch for a goal-kick. Nevertheless, Roma were offering nothing clear cut themselves and in the 39th minute Wayne Rooney dropped outside the box and spun a ball to Paul Scholes just inside the left of the box who, in turn, floated a cross to an onrushing Ronaldo, who produced a towering header to give United a 1–0 lead.

In that goal, you can see an entire football philosophy at work: Wayne Rooney drops deep and Paul Scholes runs beyond him; Park Ji-sung, as the furthest forward of the three, makes a break for the centre of the goal to become the 'striker'; Ronaldo makes the late run; and Wayne Rooney has made a run to the back post. As a result Roma are pulled all over the place when the goal goes in – Park Ji-sung has attracted three Roma players to the edge of the six-yard box, leaving Rooney unmarked at the far post and Ronaldo left to contest a header with a desperate and ultimately doomed challenge from Marco Cassetti. As the goal goes in, United have five players in the Roma penalty area six minutes before half-time, including left-back

Man Utd v Roma

Direction of Man Utd attack

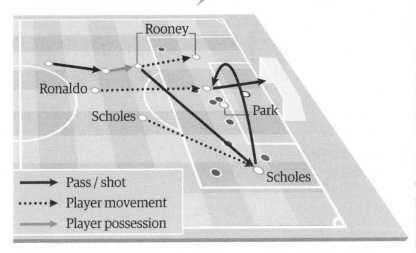

Patrice Evra. If ever you want to see how movement can disrupt even the most well-drilled top-class sides, take a look at that goal. When the ball hits the net, United have an almost perfect inverted front three.

Still Roma went after Ronaldo, constantly kicking and tugging at the Portuguese, but Ronaldo kept his cool – after giving the ball away, he won it back before unleashing a 25-yard shot that rattled the post. A second from Wayne Rooney in the 66th minute gave United an impressive 2–0 first-leg lead that they improved on with a 1–0 win at home in the return leg. But, make no mistake about it, it was the tactics and movement that won the tie.

This approach only works with highly versatile players who have a strong desire to score goals and an equal desire to win the ball back, thanks to a high work ethic. Tactically, Ferguson did not really get the credit he deserved but, if anything, his fluid front three gave him one of the greatest sides in the modern era: Ferguson had pre-empted where tactical football is in the Premier League today by at least five years.

More importantly, the approach re-established United as one of the regular favourites for the Champions League. In the big matches Ferguson would always play Park Ji-sung. In fact, my friend who played for United at the time used to tell me, 'In the big games, Park was the first player on the team-sheet – he's like a little pest who won't leave you alone. Ferguson would say to him before the game, "Get in amongst them, Ji. Nobody can live with you." And they couldn't. He loved playing him in Europe – he disrupted so many teams' shape and flow.' But Ronaldo was the star. He helped them to two finals, the first in 2007–08, which the team won, and the second in 2008–09, which they would lose. In 2008 Ronaldo won the Ballon d'Or and the following year, in the summer of 2009, Real Madrid broke the world transfer record for a player by signing him for £80 million.

Ronaldo is unlike any player that I've played against. The key to his excellent performances is being able to do everything, and more, that his contemporaries can do – but at twice the pace. And I don't mean simply sprinting up the pitch. I'm talking about his shots, which are consistently harder than anybody else's, and the way he doesn't control the ball, he drags it with him as it arrives, while his legs are just entering their first stride. Everything he does is about being on the front foot and, above all, about being direct. When he arrived at United he was intent on showing us how many step-overs he could do and how skilful he was – and the media and pundits alike complained that there was no end product.

Today, his direct approach, coupled with the fancy footwork he honed in those first couple of seasons at United (and before that at Sporting Lisbon), has ensured that defenders cannot second-guess him. When Ronaldo is running towards you at full speed – and I've been there – it is impossible to predict which way he is going to go. As a result I'd have to stop and stick a leg out – sometimes I could toe the ball, and sometimes I'd bring him down. What really used to piss me off, however, was that whenever you'd bring him down he'd sit on the ground and throw his arms in the air while looking like he was about to cry. I'd look at him and say, 'What the fuck is up with you? Never been fouled before?' Not once did he answer back, and I now know that this was because sitting on the floor was his way of counting to ten and regaining his composure.

What stands out about Ronaldo, when you play against him, is that he is an athlete: he looks like a middleweight boxer when he takes his shirt off, and yet he moves like Nijinsky, the Russian ballet dancer. When he runs away from you, he does so with the drive and determination of a 100-metre runner in the first throes of the race, and when he arrives in the box to attack a header his knees are already level with your face as you're still getting ready to jump. He is a supreme athlete, the like of which I've never played against before.

Any coach trying to drill his defenders in how to engage a player who can run with the ball will tell the back four to drop off and try to show the player towards the line. But

Ronaldo does not run down the line – he wants to follow the path that is the shortest distance towards the goal, so he runs directly at defenders and backs himself to shift the ball once they make a move towards him. It is still, to some degree, considered successful defending if a team can coax a player into shooting from 30 yards. But Ronaldo has changed that. A Ronaldo shot from 30 yards has a very good chance of finding the goal.

As with all the great players, they raise the bar with their performances. More than that, they raise the performance levels and standard of opposition players whose job it is to stop them – as well as inspiring the next generation.

THE KNOCK-ON EFFECT

You know what killed players such as Claude Makélélé, Patrick Vieira and Roy Keane, even though they could actually play? UEFA. And do you know why UEFA made it harder for them? Because players like Gareth Bale, Ronaldo and Lionel Messi are simply too exciting and valuable to the sport to allow others to kick the shit out of them. UEFA wanted all the flair players on the pitch for the showpiece tournament that is the Champions League and they don't want those players injured, so it's my belief that they have systematically encouraged referees to give out ever-easier yellow cards over the last ten years.

And I make no apologies for agreeing with them. All the bullshit that football is a man's game is just that, bullshit. Does it make the person who breaks my leg more of a man than me? I don't think it does. The evolution of forcing tackling out of the game has meant that skilful players can now blossom but, in terms of winning the ball back, it has meant that teams can play a high-energy game, pressing and hustling the opposition into mistakes in their own half rather than waiting for them to enter their half of the pitch before taking their legs away from under them. For my money, the game was far more exciting to watch because of that change. Ultimately, the skilful players, thanks to a healthy dose of commercial pressure, won out.

Winning the ball back now is nothing really to do with tackling, it is all about having athletes who can get round their opponents and force a mistake, players who are fitter, stronger and faster than their counterparts. If you look at players such as Bale, Ronaldo, Eden Hazard, Luis Suárez, Sergio Agüero, these guys are athletes – when they take their tops off they look like cruiserweights; they are fit and strong and can win the ball back without having to lift somebody off their feet in the process. It has taken a long time for English teams to cotton on to the fact that tackling is going the way of the dodo, but it will be the making of our national team, trust me.

An example of how fast players can now react in a game, both in terms of their feet and their minds, can be seen in the way that they take instructions from their teammates. When I first began playing the game professionally, I'd receive a pass along with a shout of 'turn' before the player had even made the pass. Today, we are far more aware of what's around us and the player making the pass is able to leave the call to the last minute.

Nowadays, no player would ever shout 'turn' as he plays the pass, because the picture he has in his head as he looks down at the ball changes so quickly. So a player only shouts

The best young players that you probably haven't heard of ... yet

Agustín Allione, Vélez Sarsfield, right-winger

Alen Halilović, Barcelona, attacking midfielder

Lee Seung-woo, Barcelona, striker

Adama Traoré, Barcelona, winger

Viktor Fischer, Ajax, left-winger

Sebastián Driussi, River Plate, striker

Ángel Correa, San Lorenzo, attacking midfielder

Gabriel Barbosa, Santos, striker

Dória, Botafogo, central defender

Michy Batshuayi, Marseille, striker

Juan Iturbe, Roma, attacking midfielder

Jean-Paul Boëtius, Feyenoord, winger

Memphis Depay, PSV Eindhoven, left-winger

Massimo Bruno, Red Bull Salzburg, winger

Dennis Praet, Anderlecht, attacking midfielder

Adrien Rabiot, Paris Saint-Germain, central midfielder

Hakan Çalhanoğlu, Bayer Leverkusen, central midfielder

Lucas Piazón, Chelsea, attacking midfielder

Patrick Roberts, Fulham, attacking midfielder/winger

'turn' just as the player is receiving the ball. There used to be lots of interceptions and players turning in to players because, if you shout 'turn' too early, you're pretty much telling the opposition player what the man about to receive the pass is going to do.

Top players can react quickly, their feet react quickly, their brains react quickly, their bodies follow the instruction instantly and football is all the better for it. If you do miss watching the art of somebody lifting someone else off his feet, well, there's always rugby.

THE BIG PICTURE

So the question is, how can an international side take advantage of the global market, and the way domestic football evolves, in order to produce players for its own team?

In the season of 2013–14 a young player called Adnan Januzaj broke into the Manchester United first team. He was a player of Serbian descent who had been at United since signing from none other than Anderlecht, in 2011, at the age of sixteen. He is part of a new breed of players who can play in any position across a front six, a prerequisite for attacking Anderlecht youth team players. His performances for United were so eye-catching they led to calls from Roy Hodgson, the England manager no less, to get to the bottom of whether Januzaj was eligible to play for the national team. In the event he wasn't, the Home Nations agreement stating that a player must have completed at least five years of education before the age of eighteen within the territory of the relevant Football Association. (By the way, education in football is pretty much spent in a dark office, usually at the stadium, always on a Thursday afternoon, studying Leisure and Tourism.)

None of that may seem particularly relevant unless you apply it to another facet of FA chairman Greg Dyke's sweeping changes. One of the commission's recommendations is to increase the number of home-grown players in a Premier League squad from 8 out of 25 players, to 13 of the 25 by 2020–21, a year short of Dyke's goal of winning the 2022 World Cup. If he could, Dyke would love to insert a clause into that last policy that would read 'must all be English', but the reality is that politically he must not stray down that path, and legally he'd never pull it off anyway. So how, then, can Dyke use what he's left with to win the World Cup?

Germany is a nation that immediately evokes a sense of nationalism in other nations – they are easily stereotyped by other countries, especially the British, and their favourite sporting sons are very German indeed: Michael Schumacher, Boris Becker, Jürgen Klinsmann, etc. But today's Germany is a very different place to live. While the country has always been a strategic European powerhouse, the collapse of the Berlin Wall in 1989 triggered a shift in the way Germany viewed and embraced those nations around it.

Take the Germany squad that travelled to the 2010 World Cup. Of the twenty-three players selected by manager Joachim Löw, eleven had foreign backgrounds. More than half of the outfield players were either born outside of Germany or had a non-German parent. In reality, the squad was made up of eight different countries – nine when Germany was included.

Lukas Podolski, Miroslav Klose and Piotr Trochowski were all born in Poland, Marko Marin hailed from war-struck Bosnia and Herzegovina, Serdar Tasci and Mesut Özil both have Turkish parents. Striker Cacau was actually born in São Paulo, Dennis Aogo has a Nigerian father, Sami Khedira has a Tunisian father, and Jérôme Boateng has a Ghanaian father and a half-brother playing for Ghana. And that utilisation of resources ultimately helped Germany to triumph in the 2014 World Cup final with a squad of players that also included Shkodran Mustafi, a defender born to Albanian parents.

The real benefit of these players is in how long they had played together. Take the European Championship Under-21 match between Germany and England in 2009. Of the eleven who started that game for Germany, six played in the World Cup five years later. Of the entire squad that England had at their disposal, only one would travel with the senior side to Brazil in 2014, a squad player called James Milner. Incidentally, Germany won the Under-21 match 4–1.

With fewer senior positions to fill, elite clubs will trawl the world like never before in order to find the players who can become tomorrow's superstars. And that means players will be taken at an earlier age from all corners of the globe. Before long we will become used to seeing names on the back of England shirts ending in 'vić' and 'dez'. In the face of such utilisation of resources from other countries, and the natural integration of immigrants, the England team will become a multinational side, and the Premier League, having given its full backing to the plans, will be left rubbing its hands together.

Financial matters

Revenues for the top 20 wealthiest clubs grew to **€5.4bn** in 2012–13 **8**%

Dispelling the 'I pay your wages' myth:
Revenues at Real Madrid in 2012–13

Commercial

41%

Broadcasting

36%

Match day

23%

Only **10**% of AC Milan's total revenue comes from match-day revenue

Compared with **30**% at Manchester United

and **38**% at Arsenal

Number of Facebook likes in the 2012–13 season

52.4m
FC Barcelona

21.7m
Chelsea

1.6m
Atlético Madrid

IT'S FOOTBALL, BUT NOT AS WE KNOW IT

The Commercial Game

HOW CAN WAYNE ROONEY REALLY BE WORTH £300,000 A WEEK?

Nike is the largest sportswear company in the world, with a market share of 17 per cent and total revenues in 2013 topping $25 billion. Football is fast approaching 10 per cent of that revenue ($2 billion) which, when you consider that Nike had absolutely no foothold in 'soccer' until 1994, is pretty good going. In fact, the company was forced into entering the market only because America had won the rights to stage the World Cup in the same year. These numbers are all the more impressive when you consider that technology giant Facebook posted revenues of $7.8

billion in 2013. There is serious money in sporting goods – just ask Newcastle United chairman and Sports Direct founder, the multibillionaire, Mike Ashley.

All of which means healthy competition. Behind Nike are German giants Adidas, with a 12 per cent market share and revenues of $20 billion. When it comes to football gear, the numbers are even higher: between them, Nike and Adidas account for a staggering 70 per cent of the total market. But Nike is the king of spin and tops the market share despite having competed in the same arena as Adidas for only twenty years – and in spite of the fact that they have no official commercial deal to sponsor the World Cup or the Champions League directly. For the World Cup alone, Adidas pays FIFA $70 million every four years.

Today, soccer is the fastest-growing sport in the US, and both Cristiano Ronaldo and Lionel Messi are the driving forces behind that growth. Both players are hugely popular and influential in the Spanish-speaking communities across North America, and the race for market share is almost as exciting as the annual race between the two for the Ballon d'Or. Well, it is for us football geeks, anyway.

At the heart of the rivalry are layers of fundamental competition. Today, Nike is the number-one boot brand in the world, and that includes Germany. There is no other sportswear company in the world – in fact, there are very few companies of any kind in the world – that know how to market themselves in emerging territories as well as Nike.

Both companies attribute the success of their football model to a specific product that is critical for continued growth because, unlike football shirts, which are also vital, this product is 'trend-led'; that is to say, it changes every year with the fashion before appearing on the feet of the best players in the world, weeks before being available in the shops. The humble football boot has come an awful long way since Adidas first kitted out the whole West German team at the 1954 World Cup in Switzerland. And the refinement of sports marketing has been applied powerfully since Horst Dassler, son of Adidas founder Adolf 'Adi' Dassler, realised two years later that he could also get Olympians to wear Adidas footwear if he simply gave the shoes away.

At Nike, Ronaldo is critical to the company's intentions in the race to brand our feet. In 2013, shortly after Ronaldo had won the Ballon d'Or, 250 journalists from around the world turned up in Madrid to see the World Player of the Year launch a new boot for Nike. If you want to know exactly how important Lionel Messi is to Adidas, take a trip to Adidas' flagship store in Nuremberg, not far from Herzogenaurach, where Adi Dassler began the empire that would go on to bear his name. In the store itself there are two quotes: one from the legendary Adi Dassler himself, the other from the diminutive Argentinian. In fact, in a place that could not be more of a shrine to German sporting culture, you can buy Argentina shirts with Messi's name on the back. In America, Messi is the seventh most followed athlete in the country, the first footballer to break into the top ten.

But Nike are the masters of brand building and self-advertisement, and in Cristiano Ronaldo they have a poster boy who gives David Beckham hang-ups about his appearance.

What is the one thing that kids all over the world can do to emulate their heroes? They can wear shirts with the names of their heroes on the back, and they can wear an exact replica of the boot they see them wearing on TV. They can even have their name stitched into the leather.

At Adidas, Lionel Messi wears the F50 boot, a lightweight boot made for nippy players. At Nike, Ronaldo used to wear the Nike Mercurial but today he is so valuable to Nike's play on the market that he has his very own Nike sub-brand of boot called the CTR360.

If you want to know how crucial each player is to the market as a whole, take a look at the table below, which depicts the boot that has scored the most goals in the 2013–14 season across the top four European leagues (Italy, Spain, England, Germany).

Position	Goals	Brand/Model
1	761	Adidas F50
2	740	Nike Mercurial
3	473	Nike Hypervenom
4	363	Nike CTR360
5	357	Adidas Predator

The stranglehold on the top five positions in the league is not an accident. In sixth place, the Puma Evo is nearly 100 goals behind the Adidas Predator and, in fact, eight out of the top ten boots in the list are either Nike or Adidas.

But, boots aside, kit sponsorship remains big, big business and, in some cases, critical to the appeal of the brand in a specific territory. While Adidas will officially sponsor the World Cup, Nike will dominate the shirts of the players who will be seen in every media outlet globally on a daily basis. In the year of the 2014 World Cup, the Oregon-based company sponsored the kits of ten national teams, including France, Holland, Neymar's home country Brazil, Wayne Rooney's England and Cristiano Ronaldo's Portugal. Adidas sponsored nine kits, including those of Germany, Spain and, most importantly, Lionel Messi's Argentina.

But it is another team that is perhaps the key to Adidas' pursuit of the North American market – and it has involved such a brilliant piece of marketing that even Nike are unable to do anything about it. In the 2014 World Cup Adidas sponsored the shirts of Mexico. According to the Pew Hispanic Center, there are 12.7 million immigrants from Mexico living in the USA and 31 million Hispanics of Mexican origin. When the Mexican national team plays a friendly match in the US, something it now does routinely, the stadiums are always sold out. Surely Nike would want to cash in on such a big opportunity in their own back yard? After all, emerging markets are their specialty.

The problem Nike has is that it sponsors the US national shirt, something that it is almost obliged to do. The sheer number of Mexican immigrants settling in the US has not been plain sailing, of course – the cultural landscape has changed markedly in a short space of time (in 1970 there were fewer than one million Mexican immigrants), with US jobs, neighbourhoods and education all affected. Today there remains an undercurrent of ill feeling from many Americans towards the Mexican community. All of which puts a company as quintessentially American as Nike in a rather tight spot. And, because of that, America is now the largest single market for its biggest rival, Adidas.

The most followed player in the Premier League is Wayne Rooney with

9.6 million followers

Mesut Özil is second with

7.56 million

The value of the international shirt remains huge business in other territories too. For a long time players had a boot deal, a club shirt sponsor and a national team sponsor – very often all three were different, and if two of these did marry up it was largely a coincidence.

But when Ronaldo, Messi and Rooney became brands in their own rights, thanks in no small part to the success of the David Beckham deal at LA Galaxy, and began breaking down the barriers of new markets with their global appeal, the sporting manufacturing giants of Adidas and Nike were right behind them. However, there was a problem: many of the deals in place were long term, and have only recently come up for renewal.

Wayne Rooney's situation with Nike has been the most protracted to date, and the best example of the value of a single player to both his boot sponsor, his domestic club and, of course, his national team. Nike, clearly, do not want their star players to be wearing Adidas shirts for their national team. Hence the emergence of tie-ups, known under the term of '360 deals', which are reserved for the elite players and, of course, all help to push player wages up.

To understand why wages can reach such astronomical numbers, take a look at what was happening behind the scenes when Wayne Rooney asked to leave Manchester United recently. In 2013 Nike entered an exclusive renegotiation period with United as part of their initial thirteen-year sponsorship deal, signed in 2002. The clause in the existing deal effectively gave Nike first refusal. Nike already sponsored Manchester United's star player, Wayne Rooney, who wears Nike Hypervenom boots, sold and seen all over the world thanks to his association with Manchester United, a brand that is similarly waging a marketing war on developing markets along with Nike.

In 2012, Nike had already tied up the England team in what had been a brutal example of its pursuit of key brands within football. In order to gain a larger global foothold in the Premier League, in 2007 Nike had bought Umbro, the then England team sponsors, for £285 million, and began winding down the company's contract with the FA. Behind the scenes Nike brokered a deal of their own and, in May 2012, sold Umbro to the Iconix Brand Group for $225 million; in September, the FA announced that future England kits would be made by Nike.

The England team would become Nike's answer to Adidas when it had had to concede the Mexico kit. Adidas could not be seen in Germany to be associated with the England kit for obvious historical reasons. Nike was desperate to take full advantage and tie up the first elite-player 360-deal in English football.

The crux of that deal rested at the feet of one man, Wayne Rooney, and his advisors knew it. By this point, Nike's outlay was vast, the revenues it stood to generate were enormous, and the individual brands at the heart of the deal were all global icons standing to make a fortune once the deal went through. In late summer 2013, with everything in place, Rooney's agent confirmed that his client wanted to leave the club. Again.

Cue mass panic. The deal between Nike and United stalled. Their American owners were incensed, and although United knew exactly what Rooney's motives were that didn't stop Chelsea putting in a bid for the England player to see if they could unsettle the situation further. There was no way United would allow Rooney to leave, even for a great price.

The reason was simple. Is Wayne Rooney the best player that Manchester United could have playing in the number 10 role? The answer is no, there are better players out there, cheaper players even. But with Nike's 360 deal Rooney is easily the most valuable to his club, his country and to Nike and, because he remains in England, he is the most valuable English player in the Premier League, he is the global poster boy for the Premier League, his country and his club. In short, Rooney is one of quite literally only a handful of players who directly affect United's bottom line, thanks to their global appeal.

With everybody backed into a corner, Rooney wasn't just holding the aces – he had the entire deck. Negotiations went on but under a new set of terms: the player would take a split of the revenues generated by Nike with England and Manchester United as well as his bootwear.

Manchester United pushed Nike higher on the figures in order to pay a bigger wage to Rooney. Finally, in February 2014, Wayne Rooney signed a new five-year contract with Manchester United worth £85 million.

For the first time in twenty-five years, with the deals on the table bigger than ever, the club's board sided with a player against their legendary manager, and at the end of the season Sir Alex Ferguson retired.

At the very least Nike now had a 360 deal for six months and, crucially, for the World Cup starting in June. And then Nike stunned the commercial world by pulling out of negotiations with United. Many cited the fact that United had finished seventh in the league, and that England would be something akin to a no-show in Brazil. There may be some truth attached to both of those factors but, as my man on the inside told me – a man who is one of only a few at Nike to wear a suit to work – 'The sticking point was emerging markets. We manufacture every piece of United apparel and, in emerging markets such as some areas of the Far East – but in particular Africa, where the customer can't afford the high-ticket items – we produce merchandise at a price that is affordable. It is this market where we can make profit. United wanted 50 per cent of this market and, because of that, the deal became unworkable.'

One day after the World Cup final in Brazil Adidas announced that it would pay a record £750 million ($1.3 billion) to supply Manchester United with shirts and kit over a ten-year period; a world record for a football club, and more than double the previous biggest deal – a £31 million-per-year deal that Adidas is reported to have struck with Real Madrid.

'Adidas will not make a penny on that deal,' said my suit at Nike. 'In fact, I'm telling you now that they will lose money on that deal. We are a bigger company than Adidas and we have run the numbers, and they don't work, so I'm really looking forward to seeing what happens there – while remaining very happy that we have Wayne Rooney and the England team in our stable.'

Wages are now a reflection of market forces rather than exclusively about the talent a player has. In order to secure more 360-degree deals, manufacturers are paying bigger and bigger sums to clubs and national teams and, of course, the players themselves. But where there is a looming 360 deal, there lies a rival sporting manufacturer determined to put a dent in it.

The most obvious and interesting split is the breakdown of Ronaldo's and Messi's commercial sponsorship deals. Adidas sponsor Lionel Messi's feet and his international kit, but not his club side, Barcelona – that honour is all Nike's and it means that even though Adidas quite rightly consider Messi to be one of their assets, Nike can trade off his Barcelona connections. The problem for Nike is that their own asset, Cristiano Ronaldo, is in the same boat: his footwear and his international team, Portugal, is all Nike, but his Real Madrid kit is made by Adidas.

The fact that you can see Messi's face in the Nike store in a Barcelona kit – and Ronaldo's in an Adidas store in a Real Madrid kit – is indicative of why these two players, aside from their obvious talent, are worth so much money in commercial terms. Neither Adidas nor Nike will ever let the other have a 360 deal for as long as the two best players in the world take to the pitch for the two biggest

There were

672 million

tweets sent related to the 2014
#WorldCup

teams in the world.

Lionel Messi's new five-year deal, signed with Barcelona in May 2014, is worth £16.3 million a year; a figure that even eclipsed Ronaldo's. It was the Argentinian's seventh deal in eleven years and was made possible because Messi entered into a revenue share with Barcelona for his image rights. Now, that may sound like giving away half your off-field earnings, but the reality is that a commercial management company can only get you so far – piggy-backing the brands of Barcelona and Nike can get you a lot further because, when all three combine to promote something, the deals eclipse anything that a player can do on his own. It's the brave new world and the figures are only going to go up from this point on. Ronaldo is right behind Messi: in 2013 he earned $73 million, including endorsements, and in the same year he signed a new five-year deal with Real Madrid worth £76 million.

An advertiser's dream

Player	Club kit	National team kit	Boot manufacturer
Messi	Nike	Adidas	Adidas
Ronaldo	Adidas	Nike	Nike
Rooney	Nike	Nike	Nike
Neymar	Nike	Nike	Nike
Bale	Adidas	Adidas	Adidas

Top five league attendance of European clubs in 2012–13

Borussia Dortmund
79,893

Manchester United
75,530

FC Barcelona
71,235

Bayern Munich
71,103

Real Madrid
65,268

West Ham are the 29th wealthiest club in the world with 2012–13 revenues totalling **£83.4m**

Their manager, Sam Allardyce, is the 13th highest paid manager in the world with an annual salary of almost **£3m** or **3.5%** of total revenues

Top five wealthiest clubs based on total revenues for 2012–13

Real Madrid
€518.9m

FC Barcelona
€482.6m

Bayern Munich
€431.2m

Manchester United
€423.8m

Paris Saint-Germain
€389.8m

In November 2013, just two months after Gareth Bale signed for Real Madrid for a world record £85.3 million, Adidas announced that it had secured a deal to manufacture the Welsh kit from 2014. In doing so, Bale became the latest player, in what is still only a handful of truly world-renowned stars, to be secured to a 360 deal.

WHAT ABOUT THE REST OF US?

When Adidas approached me to sponsor my boots I politely declined. I was pretty full of myself back then and didn't want to be seen as selling out. Now, of course, I wish I hadn't been so hasty in leaping to the moral high ground – because what I've come to realise is that there are no brownie points for not selling out in football, because it is expected. It is, in fact, almost demanded.

Later, I was told that Adidas had embarked on an aggressive pursuit of the top three players at the top three clubs in Europe as their new business model. They had decided to try to affiliate themselves with only the best and most commercially valuable players in the world. David Beckham was scooped up, as was Zinedine Zidane and many other stars. For a time, at least before Nike pulled their finger out, the stable of world-class talent wearing Adidas boots was awesome.

So what does that have to do with me? After all, I'm not a world-class player. Maybe not, but in order to achieve exclusiveness Adidas began to buy the remaining players – those of us who didn't shift piles of boots by the container load – out of their contracts, for an awful lot of money. My advice to anyone reading this who goes on to become a footballer is to grab commercial deals, so long as they are right for you, when they come along. The real cost to a player in selling out only genuinely reveals itself in times of hardship.

THE NUMBERS WILL ONLY GO UP

The advent of the international UEFA Nations League tournament is a prime example of the different avenues UEFA, various football associations and commercial partners are willing to explore in order to get the biggest teams and the biggest stars on to our screens on a more regular basis. Ultimately, it is a commercially led experiment that will bring in vast sums through TV deals and affiliates of the tournament when it is first played in 2018.

The league structure will be split into four groups, initially seeded, but thereafter played on a promotion–relegation basis. It is a great idea and will help younger players to get more game-time and experience at the highest level.

And it has led to some very interesting developments from companies outside of the regular TV networks that want to screen the competition. BT's move into the world of sport on TV was a masterstroke – undoubtedly when the time comes to renew the rights to live Premier League games, Sky will have some very stiff competition. It won't all come down to who puts the most amount of money on the table, because Sky has a worldwide brand and a fantastic product, whereas BT is simply not up to that standard yet – and for the board of the Premier League that is a very real point of consideration.

The most mentioned players in the 2014 World Cup were:

1. **Neymar**
2. **Lionel Messi**
3. **Luis Suárez**
4. **Cristiano Ronaldo**
5. **Arjen Robben**
6. **Oscar**

However, both Sky and BT may have far larger problems on the horizon than securing the next set of domestic rights. Almost as soon as rumours broke of a new UEFA international tournament back in September 2013, Facebook began negotiations with Oculus VR, a company specialising in virtual reality technology. The Oculus Rift headset has the potential to revolutionise not only sport but everyday life. The headset effectively allows the wearer to sit in a stadium or arena and watch the game as if they were actually there live.

Think about the potential of that kind of technology for a moment. If Manchester United installed a camera in the best seat in Old Trafford they could beam live games to anybody wearing the headset anywhere around the world, in real time. The wearer would have almost exactly the same experience as if he or she were present at the game, but all from the comfort of their own home. Now think about the commercial possibilities of a model like that if we scale it up. Premier League teams currently receive around

£60 million a year from the Premier League, via Sky, through TV rights money. But if a club such as Manchester United, with millions of fans around the world, had the chance to sell every home match to every one of their supporters, then that would blow any Sky deal clean out of the water.

And if you're watching the game in real time at home, but sharing the experience of somebody who is actually at the stadium, then advertisers might like to flash up the occasional, tailor-made adverts during play. Commercial partners, such as Nike and Chevrolet, who already pay hundreds of millions of pounds to be associated with Manchester United, could suddenly be putting deals on the table unlike anything we've ever seen before.

The potential is so enormous that clubs the size of United could, in theory, even undercut what it costs to watch football through Sky. If they charged £5 to view a game through a headset, with an average of three home games a month meaning a subscription of £15 – and they were then able to sell the best seat in the house to one million of their fans around the world for each game, and maintained that for the length of the season, that would bring in £135 million a year just from the game, without any sponsorship or in-play betting. And that's all profit.

Facebook bought Oculus for $400 million in cash and 20 million shares, which brought the deal to $1.6 billion in total. It may just be the best deal that they ever pull off. As their chief executive, Mark Zuckerberg, said in a statement when the deal was announced in May 2014, there is the very real possibility of 'completely new kinds of experiences' in communications, media, entertainment and education. 'Imagine enjoying a court-side seat at a game just by

> **Mario Balotelli** holds the record for the most re-tweeted tweet from a footballer:
>
> **'If we beat Costa Rica I want a kiss, obviously on the cheek, from the UK Queen.'**
>
> It was re-tweeted
>
> 175,845 times

putting on goggles in your home. One day, we believe this kind of immersive, augmented reality will become a part of daily life for billions of people. Virtual reality was once the dream of science fiction. But the internet was also once a dream, and so were computers and smartphones. The future is coming and we have a chance to build it together.'

But the scary thing is, the future is already here. England Rugby and their commercial partner, O_2, already offer courses, coached by former player Mike Catt, using Oculus Rift headsets that allow fans to train with the first-team squad. If enough people want to use the technology then the price will ultimately come down to, well, the price of a set-top box, perhaps?

I can hear people scoffing at the thought of the entire world suddenly buying up headsets with which to watch pay-for TV. But in order to build the various prototypes of its headsets that Oculus needed, the company turned to the crowdfunding platform, Kickstarter, for capital. Oculus eventually raised $2.4 million, ten times the amount the company had initially sought – it was a performance that ranked as one of Kickstarter's biggest successes. Clearly, the demand for this kind of technology has been around for a while, and now it just needs a company capable of giving it to the world at an affordable price, and with the right content that people want to watch. Expect to see Facebook make a big play for the world of sport in the not too distant future.

So what does all this mean for the players? Well, the more 'bums on seats' there are, the more eyeballs looking in, and the more demand for top-level football around the globe, particularly in new markets, then, ultimately, the revenue driven by commercial activity will continue to rise. That means wages will continue to increase and instead of a top club such as Manchester United having just one player on £300,000 a week it will have several, because the pressure to keep the club at the forefront of the 'entertainment dollar' will make it viable. It might not happen for ten years, but it will happen.

So, never turn down a boot deal, never do what I did and play the 'morality' card by insisting that you are some kind of artist and that your feet are not for sale to anybody except a bigger club that might want to buy you and pay bigger wages. Take whatever is on offer, provided it is the best deal on offer. If Nike offer £50,000 a year to brand your feet but Adidas offer £51,000, take the Adidas offer, because the day after you sign the deal may be your last day in football.

As much as it annoys people, especially after such a woeful display in Brazil, it is difficult to say that players who are making shampoo commercials and stuffing their face with baguettes are doing the wrong thing. After England lost to Uruguay in the second group game, my friend texted me with a typically ridiculous comment: 'Probably too busy thinking about his next TV advert to keep that one out.'

It isn't the TV adverts that are the problem; it's the fact that England aren't as good as other teams in world football.

WHY IS THE EUROPA LEAGUE DESIGNED TO HOLD TEAMS BACK?

I actually think that the underdog is a thing of the past – certainly where the neutral is concerned. Many people now want to see the best players for as long as possible, particularly in the Champions League and the World Cup. I'm reminded of an advert for the FA Cup, in which the American boxing promoter Don King sent himself up as a man selling the FA Cup on behalf of the BBC. With two Beeb execs sitting opposite him in a grand office, the King launched into a tirade of promotional patter: 'The FA Cup. What kind of name is that? You need something big like a bowl: the FA Bowl. The FA Super Mega Bowl!' The idea behind the advert was in the strapline: 'The FA Cup. It don't need no Don.' This was at a time when many people felt that the FA Cup wasn't being taken seriously – and, of course, since then corporations like the BBC have realised that a certain amount of spin is exactly what the FA Cup needed, no matter how much people wanted to believe that the famous old competition sold itself. But the real lesson from that advert lies in another pearl of wisdom that King delivered in true 'jazzmatazz' style: 'Nobody wants to see champs knocked out!'

What a young scriptwriter for an advertising agency had stumbled upon was exactly what had been missing from the FA Cup for years. More importantly, he understood where the Americans have got it so right in terms of marketing. Neutrals do not want the underdogs to win in quarter-finals and semi-finals because it means that the best players are missed in the latter stages of competitions – and neutrals supply the bulk of sporting TV audiences. For example, I watch the Ryder Cup, the Mosconi Cup, the World Snooker Championships and Formula One, and, I can honestly tell you, I couldn't give a shit who wins any of them, it's just on in the background. But, when I do cast an eye in the direction of the TV, I enjoy the sports and the skills on display, secure in the comfort that I'm watching the very best in the sport that's on.

Seeding helps to prevent big teams from falling foul of each other in the group stages of the Champions League, allowing them to go as far as possible and make as much money as possible. Take the Europa League, for example. For most teams, playing in the Europa League is a headache they could do without. My senior friends at Tottenham tell me that it is easier to lose money than make money playing in the Europa League and, furthermore, that it makes trying to qualify for the Champions League that little bit harder because it can add an extra eight or ten games – another fifth – to the season, which allows a lot of potential for picking up injuries. They all say, to a man, they'd rather be out of it. But one of them went further. He said, 'If you look at the Champions League, the teams involved get to drop out and play in the Europa League at a certain point. That keeps their earning power at a good level while giving us an opportunity to get knocked out and keep our earning potential down. Financially at least, the Europa League is designed to keep us in our place and protect the top four clubs in the major leagues across Europe by giving them as much TV revenue as possible. UEFA has even changed the financial rules so that if we could find an Arab billionaire to invest in our club, he no longer could to the extent of, say, Man City, because of the FFP [Financial Fair Play] rules. I don't understand how it is right that five years ago PSG, Man City and others were allowed to do that – and steal a march on everybody and position themselves as elite clubs – but we now can't; we are further away from them than ever. But I know why those rules came in, and it wasn't to protect the odd club that goes bust every hundred years. They were brought in to draw a line between the elite and the rest. The way the Europa League is designed is just another way of protecting the elite clubs. We don't even get a Champions League place if we win it.'

After years of pressure, UEFA finally decided to allow the winner of the Europa League to have a Champions League spot, but only to make absolutely sure that any elite club that endured a bad season, such as Manchester United, had yet another chance to make it back to the Champions League. Now, compare my Tottenham friend's sentiment with the thoughts of my friend who works at Chelsea and travels to all their European games.

'Did you know that we made no money from the Europa League when we won it? All it did was to get in the way of the other competitions we were involved in. When we won it, that was a nice feeling, but it wasn't the Champions League. The players made some bonuses from it, the fans had some good days out, but I think even they were feeling like it was a very poor second best. We're not ungrateful – it is just a competition that we don't feel we should be playing in. We should be competing to win the Champions

League every season, not the Europa League. We have to set our sights as high as we possibly can. There is no other way to go about it.'

There is no doubt that the top teams playing in the Champions League have an infinite amount of power and sway between them, and should UEFA's president Michel Platini eventually decide to run for the FIFA presidency then he will certainly be under pressure to keep them where they expect to be – if he wants to ensure their loyal support.

THIEFA: FOR THE GOOD OF OUR GAIN

There is a huge difference between a player accepting a lucrative commercial deal in a career that is finite and an organisation that likes to rub people's face in how wealthy they are while pretending that they're not. It's like the game that my son plays when he's in an annoying mood and he puts his hand as close to my face as possible and says, 'Yeah, but I'm not touching you.'

In the summer of 2014, during the World Cup finals in Brazil, only three years after promising his previous term would be his last, and in the middle of the worst bribery scandal FIFA had faced since the last one, Sepp Blatter, the organisation's president, somehow managed to garner enough support from FIFA delegates to announce that he would run for a fifth term. At the age of seventy-eight, no less.

That announcement came in the wake of stinging international condemnation of FIFA's practices surrounding the awarding of the 2022 World Cup to Qatar from FAs and sponsors alike. It was alleged that top Qatari football

During the semi-final between Brazil and Germany fans sent more than

35.6 million

tweets – a new Twitter record for a single event

official, Mohamed bin Hammam, FIFA's member for Qatar, paid out $5 million (£2.98 million) to win support for the nation's campaign to host the event.

Blatter's desperation to cling to power can be glimpsed in further comments he made in another press conference in São Paulo around the same time when he said, 'Why don't we give team managers the possibility of two challenges for refereeing during the match? If a manager disagrees with a decision, why should he not ask for an immediate TV review with the referee?'

It sounds like an idea that popped into Blatter's head while he was on stage – not unlike a comedian who's struggling to win over the audience and, with his options running out, decides to press a button on his jacket that spins his bow tie around. Blatter, after all, is fiercely opposed to innovation of any kind in football, especially technological intervention, though – with a FIFA election coming up – he did finally approve goal-line technology at the World Cup this year.

But there is always a reason as to why anybody in power holds on for so long, despite almost everything he says causing so much sustained embarrassment to his own organisation and members. Right on cue, Blatter accused the British media during the same tournament of being 'racist' in their pursuit of what he perceived to be an attempt to 'destroy' FIFA's values.

Racist? This is a man who, in November 2011, claimed that there was no racism in football – at precisely the same moment Liverpool's Luis Suárez had been officially charged with racially abusing Manchester United's Patrice Evra.

And, as for 'values', there are no values at FIFA – not values with any morals behind them anyway.

FIFA has survived for so long because it returns £3 billion to its member countries every four years – and if you know the value of supplying elite football, globally, then you will also know that a cut of £3 billion does not represent the true value of world-class football to the top European football associations either. Last season the Premier League sold its TV rights for a period of three years for a combined £5.6 billion. FIFA's chunk of change is small beer in comparison. That said, there are countries where a £3 billion slice of the pie actually goes a long way.

FIFA's members are not limited to European heavyweight nations such as England, Germany, Spain and Italy – or even the South American powerhouses of Argentina and Brazil. Member countries also include tiny nations such as Trinidad and Tobago, where the vote of former FIFA vice president Jack Warner counts for just as much as a vote from any member hailing from an elite European footballing nation when the destination of the next World Cup is being decided.

During a FIFA presidency election, a delegate from Trinidad and Tobago could be a very important and powerful ally. If you wondered why the votes of delegates such as Jack Warner are so coveted by Blatter, and why Warner appeared so close to the Swiss football president, look no further than the power that he has wielded in his home country of Trinidad and Tobago.

When Trinidad and Tobago qualified for the 2006 World Cup in Germany, the players faced the unpleasant task, as every team does at one point or another, of having to negotiate their bonuses for the competition. Warner, who was a special advisor to the Trinidad and Tobago Football Federation (TTFF), brokered the deal that would see both the players and the TTFF share in the revenues from their participation in the World Cup, as given to them by FIFA.

After the World Cup the TTFF declared total revenues of TT$18.25 million. The players rubbed their hands together – and then, incredibly, the same governing body declared costs of TT$17.9 million, which gave the players around £5000 each. All of the TTFF figures were unaudited. But such a small bonus was still enough for Warner to accuse the players of 'holding the federation to ransom because of greed'.

Later, an independent government audit would reveal that the actual figure received by the federation for Trinidad and Tobago's involvement in the 2006 World Cup was in excess of TT$173 million.

My personal disdain for FIFA and Sepp Blatter goes way back, and I will give myself away to some very senior people who know the real me with what I'm about to say – but I'll say it anyway, because it's a good anecdote.

After a phone call from *The Sunday Times*, I was told that my call-up to the England team had been confirmed and, not only that, I would be starting the next match. I had taken the call from a very good journalist friend of mine at the paper, who also told me that there would be a FIFA delegation at the game for the pre-match handshakes, rather than the usual royal party. 'Sepp Blatter will be there,' he said.

'Really?' I replied. 'I'd love to turn my back on him. Imagine that?'

There was silence for a few moments before the journalist broke it.

'Well, why don't you, then?'

The conversation went on for another hour after that, with both of us airing all the pros and cons around such action. By the end of the phone call I had decided that when Sepp Blatter got to me in the pre-match handshakes I would turn around and show him my back. Think about that for a moment. The picture would go around the world in seconds, and would make a huge point both at home and abroad. It was exciting.

Getting arrested that night is one of my biggest footballing regrets, if not *the* biggest. It wasn't that it cost me an England cap – I never harboured any burning ambition to play for England in the way that some other players do, because by the time I was due to be called up I didn't consider myself worthy of England, and all it did was annoy me and draw attention to the fact that, at the time, there was a chronic lack of world-class talent in and around the England squad.

Instead of going down in history as the first international player to make a stand against FIFA and Sepp Blatter – and a football world that was refusing to draw attention to a raft of controversies – I returned home from the police cell, switched on my phone and saw a message from the journalist. It just said, 'You idiot.'

Thankfully, football is now finding its balls. In yet another FIFA press conference in Brazil, Blatter was taken apart by Greg Dyke, the chairman of the FA, who said, 'Mr Blatter, many of us are deeply troubled by your reaction to these allegations. It's time for FIFA to stop attacking the messenger and, instead, consider and understand the message. The allegations you made about the British media when you described them as "racist" were totally unacceptable.'

Dutch FA president, Michael van Praag, then went further in the same conference, saying, 'If you look at the reputation of FIFA over the last seven or eight years, people link FIFA to bribery and corruption, to a kind of old boys' network. FIFA has an executive president and that means at the end he is responsible. Besides, he doesn't make it easy on himself. People tend not to take him seriously any more and that is not good for FIFA.'

Mohamed bin Hammam was not the first at FIFA to be accused of financial irregularity, and he will not be the last. Many will argue that FIFA are a corrupt governing body, and I will say that I expect that to be proven in time. But in the short term, it can certainly be argued that the way FIFA elects its delegates, canvasses support and, not least, supports its president, is fundamentally flawed.

At one point in Brazil Blatter was facing the biggest crisis in his sixteen years as FIFA president – a week later he had garnered enough support from FIFA delegates to announce that he is likely to stand for election once more.

How can that be?

The fact is that FIFA is rotten to the core, with members not only protecting themselves but also sponsors whose deals line the organisation's coffers. Let me give you a couple of examples.

Before the Brazil World Cup, Budweiser, one of the main sponsors of the tournament, were informed by the Brazilian government that they would not be allowed to sponsor the tournament. The reasoning was sound: alcohol-related deaths had soared among the crowd during domestic games in Brazil, and the government had passed a law banning the sale of alcohol in stadiums across the country.

Under intense pressure from FIFA the Brazilian government reversed the law and the senate passed a new, so-called 'Budweiser Bill', allowing the sale of Budweiser in every stadium for the duration of the World Cup – not only that, as part of the bill, pubs, restaurants and hotels surrounding the stadiums were all banned from serving alcohol. At the Maracanã, Brazil's most famous stadium, bars were banned from serving alcohol four hours before the game started, and had to remain closed for three hours after the final whistle. The only alcohol on sale was Budweiser, found in FIFA-approved outlets around the ground.

Why would FIFA fight so hard for Budweiser – aside from the obvious fact that the company paid a reported $50 million to become an official sponsor? Well, keep in mind that FIFA, for reasons unknown to even the most sophisticated tax experts, are exempt from any kind of taxation whatsoever and, in 2014, the Brazilian government had no choice but to write off $250 million in taxes, money that went straight into FIFA's pot. Now, you may argue that FIFA is a non-profit organisation that excludes them from taxes – apparently – but, as I write, FIFA's bank balance is north of $1 billion. Blatter calls it 'a contingency', presumably in case they ever decide to buy a planet.

But the most bizarre example of how far FIFA is prepared to go to protect their sponsors came in the 2006 World Cup in Germany, where more than 1000 Dutch fans were told to remove their orange lederhosen – sponsored by the Dutch beer, Bavaria – outside the stadium because Bavaria were not official sponsors of the tournament. The trouserless fans had to watch the match in their underpants. FIFA claimed it is entitled to defend itself against what it calls 'ambush marketing'.

Blatter can operate in this way because football has no power to rid itself of the Swiss while FIFA continues to reserve the right to vote in its own president. That leaves the elite European footballing nations with an interesting and certainly enticing plan B, which is to form a European Super League that regulates itself, before turning its attention to the international scene. In truth, nobody wants this at the present moment in time, but Blatter's blatant flouting of common decency may not leave the elite with a lot of choice. They're certainly running out of patience, finally.

EVERYTHING IS FOR SALE, FOR THE RIGHT PRICE

Benfica sold 25 per cent of David Luiz's economic rights to the Benfica Stars Fund, an investment fund – with the fund itself paying €4.5 million on a valuation of the defender at €18 million. Two years later Luiz was sold to

Chelsea for €25 million, where the Brazilian international won the Champions League and, with his stock rising, was made vice captain of the national team ahead of the 2014 World Cup in Brazil. Those of you who thought his transfer to Paris Saint-Germain, three years after joining Chelsea, was driven by the club's desire to balance the books at Stamford Bridge in the light of UEFA's financial fair play rules, think again. David Luiz's transfer to PSG for a record £50 million netted the Benfica Stars Fund £12.5 million. Between you and me, there aren't many investments around these days that return a triple mark-up in three years.

Years ago I met some people who were putting a fund together with the intention of approaching clubs and buying stakes in their players. They were starting in Italy, where the laws are more relaxed and where clubs, to this day, can buy 50 per cent of a player's registration. It is this format that helps the large clubs essentially loan money to smaller clubs that have a star player who is perhaps not yet ready to make the step up. It's a variation on the standard loan system. The trouble is, people like the ones I met are always looking to exploit the loopholes. The logic was, if a club can buy a percentage of a player, why can't a regular company buy a stake too, and trade him as an asset?

I didn't take up that offer and, years later, it became almost impossible to do as much anyway after the débâcle involving the Argentinian striker, Carlos Tevez. His performances for West Ham in the relegation-threatened 2006–07 season were critical in keeping the Hammers in the Premier League.

The problem for West Ham and Tevez was that a third party had actually owned the registration of the player during the season in which a goal from Tevez against Manchester United on the final day had kept West Ham up – and relegated Sheffield United. Premier League rules state that a club must own a player's registration. West Ham pleaded guilty and were fined a record £5.5 million in April 2007.

But there was no points deduction, and Sheffield United subsequently sued West Ham for loss of earnings – eventually settling for £22 million, but only after lawyers had argued that a full court case would see West Ham bankrupted, as they had already pleaded guilty to the offence in the previous Premier League hearing.

That embarrassment led to the FA tightening up its legislation, and the little window that once existed during which, in theory, anybody could have bought a little bit of their favourite player, has now disappeared. Who would have thought one little player from Argentina could cause so much trouble?

The most followed clubs on Twitter:

12.2 million
@fcbarcelona

12.0 million
@realmadrid

4.14 million
@arsenal

4.1 million
@chelseafc

3.9 million
@galatasaraysk

PSYCHOLOGY

Football is an incredibly complicated game. The intricacies that go into creating successful teams are vast and varied and the game has many variables – not least the human factor, and the acceptance that human beings will, eventually, make a mistake.

At the heart of the template for success in football lies a fundamental question, one that underpins every aspect of everything else that happens in and around the football club: can a manager get a squad of twenty-five players to do what he wants them to do?

In his quest to make that happen, he will call on a succession of people, budget permitting, in order to make sure that his players have everything they could possibly need. When I started playing football the support staff consisted of two coaches and a physio. Today, we have masseurs, chiropractors, sports analysts, fitness and conditioning coaches, diet and nutrition gurus, and a person holding the position that has proved a revelation in the game in recent history, the psychologist.

It took a little while for footballers to trust the introduction of psychologists, however – most of us were worried that our brains were about to be rewired and we'd never be able to get back to 'ourselves'. Once we learned that their role was to supplement what we already had and that, actually, they were human beings, some of them were, in fact, pretty cool, and their involvement in the game became a revelation.

The mental side of the game is hugely important, and psychology has finally broken into the mainstream – it has never been easier to wander into a shop and buy a book that will claim to make you happier, slimmer, better at your job, and everything in between. Last year I was returning from a trip to see a psychologist in London when I popped into a WH Smith at a train station to see how the Secret WAG book was doing. The shelves were a microcosm of the public's new-found love for mental health: eight of the top twenty books in the chart were about psychology, with two in the top three.

During my time in the game I've seen a host of mental health problems, ranging from a lack of confidence in front of goal to players who worry about everything from contract talks – typically, a time when players lose form – to more serious, deep-rooted issues. I can remember having a coffee with Gordon Strachan, the former Celtic manager, and asking him what had happened to one of his former players, who I'd heard had left the game.

I was expecting to be palmed off, but the tale he began telling me was so bizarre it's worth repeating here. He said that the team had been in the tunnel before a match and this particular player had cut the 'Carling' sponsor out of his shirt with a pair of scissors, as it conflicted with his religious beliefs pertaining to the promotion of alcohol. The match officials spotted the gaping hole in his shirt and delayed the kick-off so that the Celtic staff had enough time to persuade him to replace the shirt so that the match could start.

And it went on. Strachan told me of another occasion, when he was sat at home and received a call from the authorities, who told him that this guy had locked himself in his house, pushed the furniture up against the door and was threatening to set the house on fire. Strachan was asked to get round to the address as soon as possible and talk him out of the house. Fortunately, he did exactly that. I asked Strachan what he was thinking by this time and, with classic Strachan understatement, he replied, 'Well, at that point I began to suspect something wasn't right.'

I've worked with some excellent psychologists but some are simply in a league of their own. The Secret Psychologist is widely regarded as the best in the business – not only because he has worked at the biggest clubs in the world and with the biggest names in football, but because he continues to push the boundaries of psychology and write books about the results of his innovative techniques. Huge multinational corporations pay an awful lot of money for his genius and fly him all over the world to help to get the best from their employees.

The Secret Footballer: *If you could offer one tip to a young player to improve his mental state and ultimately his will to win, what would it be?*

The Secret Psycho: Be motivated by what you wish to achieve, not by what you wish to avoid. A question a player has to ask himself is, does he play to get the cheers, or to avoid the boos? A young player could never maximise his talent by playing within the confines of 'trying not to make mistakes'. The only way in which a young player can truly express himself is by focusing upon the end goal of 'playing to his optimum'. He must remember that the only way in which he will have a great career is to become a player who focuses on learning and development. You can win and learn nothing, or lose and learn a load about yourself that means from loss you've become better. So, winning and losing must simply be seen as equal opportunities to learn. And there is also motivation to be found in something that many people on the outside would perhaps find a bit uncomfortable, but it's OK to be motivated by money. If your primary goal is to earn £100,000 a week then the only way that you will ever reach that goal is to work hard and perform spectacularly until you have reached that point.

TSF: *If a player is having a crisis of confidence like Fernando Torres went through, how could you help him?*

The Secret Psycho: With a crisis of confidence such as that of Torres, there are several strategies. Some players would do well to detach from the situation – by thinking: you can make a mistake, it doesn't make you a mistake; you can fail, it doesn't make you a failure. When we detach the action from the person, we don't get the emotional attachment that creates a fog, which compromises our ability to learn.

Confidence is like a muscle: the more you exercise it the stronger it gets. We never lose confidence, it just gets 'covered over' with replays of times when we failed, and emotional connections to that failure.

A player who lacks confidence has got to fall back on the photo album of past successes in their head – the *Match of the Day* replays stored away in the area we call 'memory'. The mind is the best practice area in the world. You can create any playing environment and any situation. You can also zoom in and zoom out, rewind and fast-forward, slow down and speed up on any part of the picture to understand your past successes better. The only thing is that this detail, in regard to visualisation, takes practice itself.

TSF: *What is the one thing that a player can do every day to make sure that he is mentally focused?*

The Secret Psycho: Focus on the basics. When we start to ask ourselves questions in real simple terms we answer them simply too. When we get caught up in a constant diatribe of self-talk we get confused and lose commitment and focus. Think of taking a penalty. If we ATQ it (Ask the Question) we stand more chance of scoring. Ask the Question is a technique where we simply ask, 'What is my clear intention?' The answer must only ever be eight to ten words long. 'I'm going to hit the ball hard, top left.' 'I'm going to place it bottom right.'

We confuse our muscles by giving them complex instructions (either mechanical-technique focused or overly detailed) instead of very simple, clear end-goal instruction.

We speak in terms of, 'I'd like to hit the ball hard in the middle, but can't take the risk. I'd look silly if I miss this. I missed one last week. I'm not having a great game, so it would be good to score this. We're one-nil down too, blah, blah, blah . . .' It's amazing you can kick the ball at all by the time all those thoughts have gone through your head.

So, just like taking a penalty, on a daily basis we must be motivated by simple, clear instructions, which focus upon completing the basics in a committed and purposeful way.

TSF: *What are some of the most challenging problems that players have presented you with?*

The Secret Psycho: The most challenging problems have mainly been based around complicating the playing world with extracurricular activity: gambling, shagging, mates of bad influence, etc.

I think the most challenging problems are usually deep-seated. However, what I believe is that if you wish to drink less, gamble less, stop biting your nails, stop smoking, get on better with the in-laws and get fitter, people think you have to work on these things separately. You have to 'cure' one and move on to the other.

But I think these are not the disease, they are the symptoms. There is one thing that changes everything.

There is a root cause, a 'one thing' that makes all the others happen. My advice is to find the one thing that changes everything.

TSF: *Is there any part of football that you can predict just by studying what people are likely to do?*

The Secret Psycho: Penalty shootouts may appear random, but enough time has now passed for us to study what players are likely to do, particularly goalkeepers. Psychologists have now studied shootouts from World Cups and European Championships between 1976 and 2012, and they've found that after three kicks in the same direction, keepers almost always dive the opposite way for the next penalty, regardless of who steps up to take it. So, if you happen to be the fourth penalty-taker then you should always stay to the side where the previous three penalties were struck.

It is the same principle as a coin toss. If somebody tosses a coin and has three heads in a row they will mistakenly believe that the next flip is more likely to be a tails. The reality is that every toss is a 50–50 chance, regardless of the length of any sequence. This is known as 'the gambler's fallacy', and is why the house always wins. Human beings appear to be of free will, made up of random decisions, and that is precisely what makes them predictable.

TSF: *What continues to surprise you in football?*

The Secret Psycho: How insecure the best players are. I have literally had to tell the best players in the world how good they are. Perfection is an asymptote. It is never achieved, and only two things ever happen when people go looking for it. Either they live unhappy lives because they are unable to find it, or they think they've found it and then worry every day that they are going to lose it.

PLAYERS WILL MAKE MISTAKES – IT'S HUMAN NATURE

When I look back at some of my antics on and off the pitch it's all I can do not to cringe at myself. I was known for despising trips abroad – the way I saw it, it was bad enough being in a regimented group of people every day of the year, but it was another thing to be away from your home comforts with them, trapped in a room or on a bus or eating together for an entire week.

'We're going where? Dubai? How long for? Why?' I hate going away with football teams; it isn't anything like a holiday. For the most part it is a mundane experience. But it is the sheer rigidness of the whole experience – when to get up, when to eat, when to talk, when to go to the toilet – there is no free will on these trips, believe me. And yet now, when I write about these wonderful places that I've visited, I do it in a way that suggests I'm eternally grateful to have had the opportunity – and I am. But for me, the football always came first, and I would always be the player who asked the questions: is this going to help us? Should we be going? We're on a good run, should we be doing anything to disrupt it?

Who'd be a manager? You're damned if you do and damned if you don't. Foreign trips are usually worth the effort, from the point of view of recharging the batteries, even if the thought of it sends shivers up my spine. It's a tough one to explain, but a break from the norm and the depressiveness of an English winter is undoubtedly a good thing, no matter how many players get arrested.

But these trips can bring out the worst side of a young player. They generally toe the line and stay out of the way, but every inch of their body is screaming at them to get involved. They want to throw on their best white T-shirt of a half-naked lady, their best chino shorts and their newest pair of Havaianas, and hit the town to explore the potential. In the worst cases they lose all sense of direction and the reason that they wanted to play football in the first place. I've seen a lot of kids come unstuck on pre-season tours, and the ones who don't generally get it when they arrive back in the UK.

When my friend James Morrison punched his West Brom teammate Saido Berahino (twice) he wasn't hung out to dry by his fellow players, for two reasons. One, he wasn't Wayne Rooney, and, two, some people in the game thought that Berahino had it coming, for the worst thing that any young kid can become is what we call in the trade 'big time' – that is to say, a young lad who has come into the first team, played a few games, done well, been written about, and it's all gone to his head. Needless to say, Berahino didn't see it that way, and reportedly threatened to sue Morrison.

There are certain things that a young player can do to help himself, though: don't give it the big one where possible, don't be too busy, don't pretend that you know everything, and don't tell the world about how much money you have and who you know. Most of them cannot wait to tell the world about the trappings of football rather than the meaning. I'm reminded of a conversation I once had with Liam Gallagher, who said to me, 'The Secret Footballer don't name-drop, man. It ain't cool, know what I mean?' And I never have.

IT WILL BE LOVE AND HATE WITH THE FANS, SO JUST ACCEPT IT

For all the books written about football, for all the information available online, and for the closeness that it is still possible to feel to the players in some areas of the country, the fans will never really know how a player feels when he steps on and off the pitch, what it's like to score, what it's like to win a football match, and how it feels to have 80,000 people watching what you're about to do with the ball.

The fans work all the hours that God sends so that they can spend part of their income on an expensive ticket to watch us play for the sum total of ninety minutes, and most of them aren't overly bothered about any problems that a player may have outside of those ninety minutes. In fact, most of the fans I talk to, including many of my friends, believe that the right amount of money will remove any problem a footballer may have. While it is true that monetary problems are generally squashed in the womb, many of the other problems everybody has to deal with in everyday life persist. We're not all that different.

And it isn't really a surprise that some fans can't get on board with that. The level of passion they feel for their local club will always evoke a sense of belonging that foreign players, in particular, should never be able to feel – unless a foreign player comes to the club and plays well, of course, then he becomes an adopted son. Football provides fans with a sense of passion like no other pastime I know of, and every now and again it blows up on all sides.

When Mark Viduka played for Middlesbrough he found himself – where the fans were concerned – in a tight spot. When things were going well he was their best hope for another season in the Premier League, but when things were going badly he was the unacceptable face of inflated footballers' wages, paid with fans' hard-earned money by a chairman in pursuit of exactly the same goal.

In one particular game, things – as you might expect with a club like Middlesbrough – were not going according to plan. The team were losing 0–2 to Aston Villa when Viduka was taken off at half-time. The announcement led to frustrated jeers by the home fans. I've seen it a million times before – it is the insatiable and totally irrational need for people who know next to nothing about football to reduce the game to a primeval and nonsensical rationale so as to have some flimsy foundation upon which to demonise their own come Monday morning. In short, the need for a scapegoat is as pressing as the need of an ex-teammate of mine to have sex with as many different women as possible.

As the tall Australian walked toward the side of the pitch the boos grew louder, until Viduka had taken his seat on the bench, where he was then faced with the fans abusing him from all sides. As the stadium erupted with all eyes on the centre-forward, Viduka, looking dead ahead as he sat on the bench, began to sing the Monty Python classic

'Always Look On The Bright Side Of Life', complete with the whistling. Needless to say, it didn't go down well with the Riverside faithful.

When the game had finished and Middlesbrough had duly lost, the players made their way out to the car park. The players' cars at Middlesbrough, for some inexplicable reason, are parked right opposite the main stand and protected by a waist-high, makeshift, metal fence, patrolled by two security guards. It isn't that anybody is daft enough to try to steal the cars, it's the fact that in Middlesbrough there isn't a lot of money about and when the team loses a football match, the people don't really want to be confronted with £100,000 sports cars ten minutes after the final whistle of a game in which they have been played off the pitch.

At £60,000 a week, Mark Viduka was the highest earner at Boro at that time and, as he left the ground, he walked into a barrage of abuse from fans who had congregated around the metal barriers protecting the gleaming cars within.

As he walked into the enclosure, a group of fellas began to get very vocal and aggressive, before one rather portly gentleman did his best to bring about early onset cardiovascular disease by abusing Viduka and all he stood for at the top of his voice: 'I pay your fucking wages, Viduka.' As he got to the car, Viduka put his bags down and started walking towards the four-foot-high metal fence a group of thirty or forty fellas were pretending to have a great amount of difficulty in scaling.

'You pay my wages?' said Viduka, looking the biggest fella dead in the eye.

'That's fucking right,' said the ringleader.

And with that Viduka extended his hand and said, 'Fair play to you, mate. You must be one rich fucker.'

And that's when you know it's time for everybody to go home without saying another word. Apparently, they still talk about it up at Boro.

The problem with a lot of fans is that they want to let off steam; they want to vent frustration. It's in their blood, they can't help themselves – they seem to get a serotonin rush from deriding others at football matches. In one of the best scenes from the film *Fever Pitch*, an Arsenal fan, an old boy, sat in a café and said, 'They were fucking rubbish last year and they were fucking rubbish the year before. I don't care if they're top – they'll be fucking rubbish this year too, and the year after that.'

That scene was shot to reflect the 1971 season, a year in which Arsenal won the double for the first time. At the end of his rant, the old boy turns to a kid enjoying his first-ever football match and says, 'Here, have a look at the number 8 this afternoon, John Samuels his name is. Remember his face, then, if you should happen to bump into him, tell him to sod off to Spurs.' And that, in a gloriously perfect scene, is how footballers understand football fans. As far as they're concerned, we're damned if we do and we're damned if we don't.

Some people are so stupid that they have no idea how stupid they are. Professor of psychology at Cornell University, David Dunning, argues that in order to know how good you are at something, it requires exactly the same skills as it does to be good at that thing in the first place – which means if you're absolutely no good at something at all then you lack exactly the skills you need to know that you're absolutely no good at it. Understand?

But don't take my word for it. Dunning, and his accomplice at Cornell, Justin Kruger, were awarded the 2000 Nobel Prize in Psychology for their efforts and that carried a £1 million reward. I could have proved their theory after just one trip to Middlesbrough, where expectation and reality are at least ten thousand light years apart. It's difficult to tell exactly who is stupid. It's at times like this that I feel extremely religious.

MAKE PSYCHOLOGY WORK FOR YOU

The problem, of course, is that wherever there are decent intentions and a strand of science that can really help people to get on in life, there are other people who are quite prepared to bend the rules for their own ends.

One of my heroes, an eminent psychologist called Stanley Milgram, was fascinated by human behaviour and, in particular, why seemingly regular people would follow orders – very often from people they've had no previous relationship with. 'How is it possible,' asked Milgram, 'that ordinary people who are courteous and decent in everyday life could act callously, inhumanely, without any limitations of conscience?' Milgram called it 'obedience to authority'.

The world of football went into meltdown when Luis Suárez bit the shoulder of Giorgio Chiellini in the 2014 World Cup. The papers were full of headlines calling for Suárez to seek psychological help; after all, this was the third time that the Uruguayan had taken a bite out of a player in only four years.

However, those of us who know about the murky world of football understand that, as long as a player has a good agent, then he can utilise every trick in the book in order to get his own way. He has convinced his mind that the agent has his best interests at heart, and will always do the right thing for him. In order to help the agent achieve the player's reward, the player will do anything he can think of that might help him.

In November 2010 Suarez bit a player while playing for Ajax. Two months later he got the move he was after when Liverpool brought him to England. In April 2013 he bit the Chelsea defender Branislav Ivanović. This time Liverpool called his bluff and their owner, John Henry, released a statement saying that Suárez would not be allowed to leave. But with time running out for Suárez to force his move through, he bit Chiellini on the shoulder in front of a billion people, and this time, as much as they would have wanted to, Liverpool simply couldn't defend him. He moved to Barcelona on 11 July 2014 for £75 million.

The point is that the football world fell for it. Despite the fact that Liverpool had one of the best psychologists in the game in Dr Steve Peters, already in the building talking to Suárez – and despite the fact that Suárez has a track record of either signing a new contract or getting a move to a bigger club every time he gets into trouble, commentators, pundits and journalists alike concluded that a person who bites somebody three times has a serious psychological problem.

Actually, thinking about it now, it's probably the greatest bit of reverse psychology that the sporting world has ever seen. Either that, or Suárez is the finest psychologist of modern times.

But there is another theory in psychology, which argues that the only way a man can become famous without talent is through martyrdom. And while Suárez is supremely talented, well, I suppose football would be a type of martyrdom, wouldn't it?

FORMATIONS

People have talked about formations for over a century. There are entire books dedicated to how some of the game's greatest-ever sides have set up and there are countless newspaper articles, including mine, talking about formations that are now nothing more than chip paper. But at the highest level, the fact of the matter is, most of the top sides have never been more fluid. For example, I've seen formations such as 4–3–3, which becomes a 4–5–1 when defending and 4–4–2 becomes 4–4–1–1 when defending with the striker picking up the holding midfielder. And some teams are playing what is more or less a 5–1–4 in their own half when they are defending, in an attempt to keep out the big guns. In other words, some formations aren't worth the whiteboards that they're drawn on.

I probably know over a dozen managers who believe that formations, in the most rigid sense of the meaning (say, 4–4–2) and particularly where attacking players are concerned, are dying out. They are being replaced with six attackers who can fully interchange positions while being joined by ever more adventurous full-backs. But that isn't to say that formations have died out altogether. In fact they've never been more varied.

Below are the most popular formations in the modern game and I will show you how today's teams are changing the way they play thanks to a revolution in attacking football. You will see that the modern-day full-back has gone from being the most dispensable player in a squad, with wages that reflected that, to one of the most sought-after and important positions within the first eleven.

WHAT WORKS AND WHAT DOESN'T

4–2–3–1

The most in-vogue formation in modern football, the key to this formation is to employ two deep-lying centre midfielders who are comfortable enough on the ball to start attacks but are savvy enough in terms of their starting positions to break up opposition attacks. The starting position for every player is hugely important. Knowing where you are in terms of your team shape is all-important because it gives a player the confidence to spring forward from the sanctuary of his 'hole' into positions that put pressure on the ball. You have to know that your team has moved position and compensated for your foray behind you, however, and you need to be absolutely sure that you have stepped out at the right time. It takes hours and hours on the training pitch to learn and quite frankly it's the most mundane training session in the history of mankind.

You can have either of the two sitting midfielders go forward when the team is attacking but one must always sit. A good example of the two deep-lying midfielders can be seen in the Liverpool side of 2013–14, in which Steven Gerrard would invariably stay put while the younger legs of Jordan Henderson would spring forward whenever Liverpool attacked. When the team were defending, they both sat in front of the back four and when the team won possession back one would make a dummy run forward, literally to get out of the way, while the other, usually Gerrard, would form a triangle with the two centre-halves so that they had an 'out ball'. An 'out ball' is the first pass forward that a team makes after winning the ball back from the opposition. It is given supreme importance in modern-day football because it can be the difference between simply defending an attack and starting one of your own. With a very good number 10, an out ball can be the most valuable weapon in a team's armoury, providing of course that it has a centre-half who doesn't panic when he's in possession of the ball and the opposition are all around him. If you were wondering why there is a shortage of top-class English centre-halves, the reason is that foreign defenders are the ones who don't panic; they are trusted on the ball and managers know that they will look forward once they have won the ball back with confidence and authority. There is always a reason for a lack of a particular positional player coming through our academies, and where centre-halves are concerned it's because we no longer want the John Terrys of this world, who simply throw themselves in front of the ball. We want players who can actually play, players who actually start attacks.

Strengths: Both full-backs can get forward at the same time, and the team can attack in numbers with up to eight players at any one time. In order to pull this formation off with the maximum effect, the team must control the midfield on both sides of the halfway line, as this allows for an extra pass in midfield. In short, the opposition cannot get near the ball. The overload in football is a much-fabled thing but for my money there is no point in overloading the pitch in certain areas today. For example, for years coaches taught full-backs to overload the wide areas in order to get a cross in. We now know that crossing the ball is a lottery, a coin toss, something that is in the lap of the gods.

The beauty of this formation is that it allows players to have a certain amount of free will, and with free will comes a multitude of headaches for the other team. It is no coincidence that Bayern Munich signed Robert Lewandowski – no doubt that he is a great goalscorer but with the way that Munich play, it is easy to see that he fits in perfectly with their ethos. At Borussia Dortmund, Lewandowski would drop deep and invariably the centre-half would follow him, at which point Dortmund's designated wide men, Reus and Aubameyang, would come inside and overload the space.

At Bayern Munich, Arjen Robben and Franck Ribéry are even better at doing this and they allow the formation to reach the next step by playing on the opposite side of the pitch to their preferred foot. Inverted 'wingers' are now the 'in thing' in football and in no formation is it better suited than 4–2–3–1. With quick players running across the pitch into space instead of down the wing into a dead end, the full-backs can now fill that space; it creates an overload of players and further options for the attacking team, and it is incredibly difficult to deal with.

The aim of the formation from an attacking point of view is to separate the defending team's defence from its midfield as early as possible. Nobody knows who to mark so nobody gets marked. Instead, the defending team resorts to sitting deeper and deeper so that it doesn't have to chase the players around the pitch and when that happens goals are only round the corner. It is the sole reason that you see some teams playing so close to the opposition's penalty area while other teams simply can't do it. Last season Bayern scored 119 league goals, seventy-two of which came in the first twenty-four games. They had more possession in last season's Champions League than any other team. They also went forty-nine games unbeaten. It's all about overloading the opposition with players who appear to be fluid but on closer inspection are actually playing to a predetermined system.

Weaknesses: The formation is very vulnerable to quick counterattacks down the sides, as proven brutally by Real Madrid in the semi-final of last season's Champions League, in which Bayern Munich were ruthlessly exposed by Real Madrid's lightning-quick Ronaldo. Generally speaking, the two centre-halves do not want to go outside the width of their 18-yard box so if both full-backs have gone forward, the holding midfielder has to be perfectly positioned, otherwise he does not have enough time to track back into the wide areas.

Also the full-backs have to be incredibly fit because they are being asked to effectively play as wingers too.

The system can be vulnerable to a more direct style of play from a team that has a strong centre-forward. The perfect example came in the 2013–14 Premier League match between Liverpool and Chelsea. The match was totally dominated by Liverpool but their performance was undone by Chelsea's direct style of play and refusal to commit men forward to support a strong centre-forward, which they had in Demba Ba.

3–5–2

Strengths: Wingbacks are key to the success of this formation. Ask any centre-half if they prefer playing in a two or a three and invariably they will say that playing in a three is easier because two are designated to mark and one plays almost as a 'sweeper'. Generally speaking, the designated sweeper will always be the player who is most comfortable on the ball.

But not all teams play with the sweeper. Some will play with an inverted three with one sat ever so slightly in front of the other two. That formation would go on to become 4–1–4–1, which came about because attacking teams began to play with only one striker and a number 10, so three centre-halves were seen as a waste. The beneficiaries of 4–1–4–1 were players like David Luiz, who can now play just in front of the two centre-halves, and any player who can do the role well now has a significant value attached to him. PSG paid £50 million for David Luiz in the summer of 2014 and, believe me, they wouldn't have paid that if Chelsea had only played him as a centre-half for two years.

A strict 3–5–2 formation was something of a rarity for many years until Holland experimented with it in pre-World Cup warm-up matches in what many saw as a way of saving energy ahead of the games in the stifling heat of Brazil. In fact, Louis van Gaal adopted the formation because there is a chronic shortage of top-class Dutch full-backs. But the formation does help to conserve energy and the only players exerting something close to their full capacity are the wingbacks, who are very often attacking players. A lot of my friends in the game argue that full-backs are basically wingbacks anyway these days, so they ought to be the fittest players on the pitch.

Weaknesses: The demise of 3–5–2 came about when teams stopped playing 4–4–2 and went to a conservative 4–5–1. The wingbacks in a 3–5–2 can become hopelessly exposed at times, which means that the two outside centre-halves need to be comfortable with going into areas that they wouldn't normally go to – which many are not. Centre-halves do not want to go into the wide areas to cover because they struggle to defend against typical wingers.

In Holland's match with Mexico in Brazil, the Dutch were poor, although the Mexicans were not much better. The conditions were tough – the competition had its first official 'cooling break' thanks to temperatures of 38.8°C and the 70 per cent humidity – but this was not the reason that Holland played with three at the back. The truth is, the Dutch squad lent itself to a 3–5–2 formation. Sometimes as a manager you have to manipulate the players at your disposal into a formation that enables the team to play at their best as a whole.

The Dutch came within a whisker of losing the game as the Mexicans simply sat back and condensed the space. It took eighty-seven minutes for the Dutch to muster a decent chance. Fortunately for them, Wesley Sneijder took it and the Mexicans fell apart, eventually losing the game to a 93rd-minute penalty. The truth is, 3–5–2 is fairly easy to counteract if a team simply sits back and nullifies the threat of the wingback. But if a team sets up to play, as Spain did, then the pace of players like Arjen Robben becomes the formation's biggest asset.

4–3–3

Strengths: A similar formation to 4–2–3–1 in terms of how it works, with two full-backs getting forward at every opportunity. Of the three in front of the back four, one will always sit and that is almost always the same player who generally plays in the middle of the three. The other two are basically box-to-box players. Many teams adopt this formation: PSG played 4–3–3 last season, as did Real Madrid at times. The manager needs to have the right personnel to pull it off. The holding midfielder has to be very, very strict, and the point man – in the case of PSG, Zlatan Ibrahimović – has to be very clever because it is his job to pull the centre-halves deep while bringing other players into the game.

The box-to-box players are important because two of the front three, the two either side of Ibrahimović, will also be crossing the ball occasionally. This means that the furthest away from the ball becomes a second striker in the box with one of the box-to-box players making a late run. It sounds easy to play in but, actually, to do it well takes know-how and discipline and incredible fitness.

Weaknesses: I never liked playing in a 4–3–3 formation because the team with which I was playing at the time did so with a flat back four, which meant that we had six players over the halfway line who were strung across the pitch and isolated from one another. This led to huge gaps appearing once the opposition had won the ball back with our players struggling to get to an opponent to close him down.

The formation only works if a team has adventurous full-backs, otherwise you're playing an attacking game of five against eight or even nine. With adventurous full-backs pushing forward, the two banks of three are squeezed into the pitch and you find that rather than trying to thread 20-yard passes into a striker or across the pitch, you're actually now playing 10-yard passes and the whole thing becomes faster and less easy for the defending team to get a handle on. It's at this point that the two banks of three can start to interchange. Without the presence of two highly energetic full-backs, the whole system is undermined.

4–4–2 IS DYING

Probably the most well-known formation of all, 4–4–2 remained popular across the world for as long as it did because it had partnerships all over the pitch – great Premier League front partnerships like Phillips and Quinn, Yorke and Cole and Sutton and Shearer. In midfield there were incredibly talented partnerships such as Keane and Scholes, Petit and Vieira and Gerrard and Alonso. But there are more intricate relationships in a 4–4–2 formation: full-backs and wingers also have a very entwined relationship, the best example of which was David Beckham and Gary Neville. Beckham would rarely go to the by-line because his fantastic crossing ability worked best when he delivered the ball from level with the 18-yard box and slightly inside from the touchline. This meant Neville could overlap him and, if the pair lost the ball while Neville had overlapped, Beckham would assume the right-back responsibilities. It's an understanding that usually comes from years of playing together.

And players were never isolated in a 4–4–2 formation. The idea behind it was that wherever the ball was, there were always at least two players around it, either defending the other, from the forward line right through to the back. And they attacked together by overlapping or backing a winger up with support. Great partnerships are formed because what one player can't do, the other one generally could.

The demise of the 4–4–2 formation came about as teams began to flood the middle of the pitch, overloading the midfield and sacrificing their width. Technically superior passers of the ball were able to manipulate attacks with greater speed and slice teams open that were now outmanned. The only way to counter it was to match the formation. The attacking threat of a five-man midfield outgunned that of two wingers and two strikers in a 4–4–2 formation. Off the back of this change, a new era of strategies and formations in football was born.

That change initially saw the demise of the winger and there are some commentators who insist that wingers remain a dying breed. They have been replaced with adventurous full-backs and talented attacking midfielders who drift into wide areas. With wingers out of the picture, the defensive shackles from the old-fashioned full-back were removed and they can attack almost at will. Today, full-backs are the starting points for many attacks and very often they are among the most physically fit in the team. And that is why Manchester United signed an eighteen-year-old from Southampton with fewer than seventy professional starts for £30 million, a world record for a teenager.

THE BARCELONA EFFECT

The team that Barcelona produced from 2008–2012 is widely regarded as the finest team ever assembled –

certainly in my house it is. It had the best players, playing the best football, with the best individual player ever and the best ideals. The club's famed La Masia academy has produced players of world-class talent, players who have won every honour the game has to offer at both domestic and international level, with its prodigies, Xavi Hernández and Andrés Iniesta, becoming two of the most decorated players of all time.

In short, Barcelona changed the face of football. Joan Laporta took the building blocks put in place by the legendary Dutch master Johan Cruyff and instilled them into every facet of the club's strategy upon his election to club president in 2003. Through Laporta's first managerial appointment, Frank Rijkaard, Barcelona were able to dominate the game thanks to the innovation of some traits that are now so common that you'd be forgiven for thinking they've been around forever.

Rijkaard began to play with a front three pressing system, which would bring them success and go on to be adopted as a template by managers all over the world. The idea behind the front three is to encourage the opposition to play out from the back and then press the ball until the team lose it by being dispossessed or misplacing a pass or by passing back to the goalkeeper, who then launches it forward (which generally ends up back in the possession of Barcelona).

LAYING THE TRAP

The trap is set by the front three players when the opposition have a goal-kick. The goalkeeper plays the ball to one of his split centre-halves who maybe passes it out to his full-back. Almost always the full-back will pass the ball back to the centre-half because the defending team has eleven men behind the ball and there is no space to pass into. The moment the ball is passed backwards the front three spring forward from their starting positions. We call this 'the trigger'. Two things generally happen at this point: the centre-half panics and kicks the ball long or passes back to his keeper who does the same, usually conceding possession, or he is robbed of the ball in a very dangerous area of the pitch.

The positions of the front three are not predetermined. They are vague, and come from experience of where to stand rather than pinpoint placement. But this is something that almost every team playing against a side that play out from the back will work on in training as a sure-fire tactic for winning the ball back. Today, lots of teams employ this tactic: Chile did it brilliantly in the World Cup and, closer to home, Southampton were superb in their closing down and pressuring of Liverpool at Anfield in the 2013–14 season.

Sometimes a team will be extra patient and wait for the back four to pass it around between them. This is almost lulling the team into a false sense of security and it encourages one crucial thing to happen. Players want to get involved in the passing and the first man to do this is generally the holding midfielder. He drops in and the centre-half or full-back passes him the ball. That is the trigger for the whole team to spring forward. Some teams prefer to wait for the holding midfielder to get on the ball rather than springing forward after the full-back has passed the ball back, because the midfielder has his

Laying the trap – Germany v Brazil

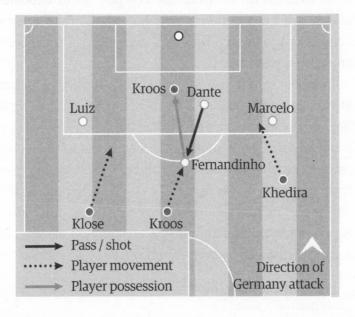

back to the opposition. How many times have you seen a holding midfielder get robbed of the ball because he either receives a bad pass and needs an extra touch or he turns in to trouble or he panics? A great example can be seen in Germany's demolition of Brazil in the 2014 World Cup, when Toni Kroos robbed Fernandinho in a dangerous position, played a one-two with Sami Khedira and duly scored. We call this 'laying the trap'.

MANIPULATING THE OPPOSITION

At Barcelona, players such as Dani Alves, Xavi, Iniesta and Messi don't only know what they should do at any given moment, they also know what their teammates are going to do. What marks them out as exceptional is that they have been coached to tell what the reaction of an opposition player will be depending on what type of ball they are about to play. In fact, they can influence the positions of opposition players.

The best example of all three of these coming together at once is when Messi or Alves is out on the right wing and Xavi or Iniesta are inside the pitch on the ball facing them. It looks as if one of the midfielders is going to play a simple pass to the wing but what you can't see is that actually both Xavi and Alves are peripherally watching the opposition's left-back. The moment the left-back takes a step towards Alves, the Brazilian runs outside him, and Xavi then plays a reverse pass in between the left-back, now hopelessly

Stay narrow

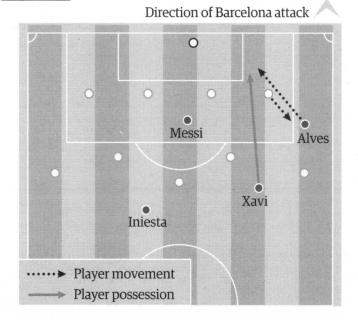

out of position, and the left-sided centre-half. This is the reason that at academy level every full-back is taught to 'stay narrow'. The moment he begins to stray towards the winger, gaps appear, and it is these gaps that Barcelona are so brilliant at exploiting.

And that is the purpose of moving the ball around the pitch: it isn't simply to keep possession for its own sake, it is so that eventually an opposition player will lose concentration and, as a result, lose his shape. Exploiting these situations doesn't just depend on having players who are acutely aware of when these opportunities present themselves; it's also about having players who can influence what the opposition players will do when the ball is in a certain position to create the chance in the first instance.

The genius of this move isn't all in the execution, though that is impressive, it is in the fact that Barcelona are directly influencing the movement of the opposition. Former Chelsea and Spurs coach, André Villas-Boas, once said, 'There are more spaces in football than people think. You can provoke the opponent with the ball, provoke him to move forward or sideways and open up a space. But many players can't understand the game.'

Playing the opposition's game for them isn't new, it has just evolved to a new level thanks to no other team in the modern era than Barcelona and the desire from the Barcelona players to improve their game.

It is this trait that elevates them from a team that is aimlessly going from side to side to a team that is manipulating its opposition into the position it wants them to be in, before ruthlessly exploiting them. It is incredibly hard to spot – I'm tempted to say impossible unless you've played – but the fact of the matter is that somebody watching Barcelona, or any top team for that matter, on the TV at home won't be able to see the eye movements and the little nods of the head and the almost telepathic understanding that certain partnerships on the pitch have. Other footballers can't even see it on TV because we are watching the same live footage. The only reason that we know what is really happening is because, to a much lesser extent, we have similar partnerships with our own teammates, we have the same 'triggers'. But Villas-Boas is right; most players do not understand the game in this level of detail and, sadly, most don't want to because they are in a comfort zone.

It is all about being comfortable with the ball at your feet. The English kids coming out of English academies haven't yet grasped that, or, rather, they haven't been coached to realise that. Everything about them when they play a one-two, something that by and large stays with them throughout their career, screams 'rush it'. English players are so scared of dwelling on the ball, they are scared that they will be tackled, they are scared that their teammates will shout at them for not moving the ball quickly enough and they are particularly scared that the crowd will collectively scream at them. At Barcelona every player to come out of the fabled La Masia academy is totally at ease with the ball.

The panic that embodies English footballers is there for everybody to see in most of the things they do, and one of the easiest ways to spot it is in a simple one-two. Conversely, it is one of the best ways to spot great technical players who are comfortable on the ball and have good knowledge of the game. Any footballer who is confident enough to wait for a player to close him down before releasing the ball knows how to play the game. Panic and game know-how are two of the biggest challenges threatening any future success that the England team may have, and while many argue that the Barcelona philosophy doesn't translate to the Premier League, there are parts of their game that we can borrow.

THE GENIUS BEHIND THE ONE-TWO

The Barcelona president from 2003 to 2010, Joan Laporta, led a revolution in the way the club operated on and off the pitch, only it wasn't a revolution in the truest sense of the word. Laporta's revolution was radical for dipping back into the club's history books by almost fifteen years and drawing on the football philosophy of previous manager Johan Cruyff, who as manager of Barcelona won four consecutive championships from 1991 as well as the club's first European Cup in 1992.

Laporta identified one crucial remnant from that great Barcelona side. He noted that every time Barcelona attacked the opposition, they did so with short, sharp passing before, at any given moment, a one-two set off a domino effect of a two-touch game that ultimately led to a shot on goal. 'Our football philosophy was based on Cruyff's mentality and his way of understanding the game, playing "two touches" and then attacking,' said Laporta.

When Frank Rijkaard was sacked by Laporta after reportedly losing the dressing room and, in particular, Ronaldinho, he brought in Pep Guardiola. This decision was based on what the former player was achieving with Barcelona B, which Laporta had realised was the incarnation of the Cruyff strategy. Pep Guardiola would take the Barcelona philosophy to a whole new level and influence teams around the world.

It is true to say that it is easier to trust a world-class player with the ball but there are reasons for that. It is the intricate details in football that ultimately make the biggest difference to a result. The fine lines are actually know-how not ad-libs. And I'll give you an example of one of the most basic moves in the game and the difference between two footballing cultures – one that knows how to use it and the other that hasn't quite grasped it.

The one-two is a potent weapon when used correctly, but its efficiency is not just in passing and getting it back. That is the bare minimum. The layers of a one-two highlight the difference between nations that are comfortable on the ball and those, like England, that panic. If you watch Lionel Messi or Andrés Iniesta you will see that they wait for the defender to commit himself to closing them down before they play the first pass. They don't play the ball for a one-two unless an opposition payer has broken ranks and is on the front foot coming towards them; it is so much easier to wait until the player does that than it is to try to play a one-two with no pressure on you. It is easier to run past a player who is coming at you than it is to give them a five-yard head start in a foot race.

Once in these promising positions, the tempo changes and the speed of execution is everything. No team managed this better and for longer than Barcelona did from 2006 and, personally, I have never seen a team create so many chances from one-touch play around the box. The point is that the game does not need to be played at breakneck speed all the time – occasionally it needs a considered approach. The team is a fluid, living, breathing beast that can collectively influence the decisions of other teams; it can't do that if everything is always 100mph. Barcelona encapsulate a team that can skilfully build up the play with precise, effective passing before exploding into fast, intricate passing moves around the box that generally lead to a host of chances.

WHAT HAVE BARCELONA EVER DONE FOR US?

Five years ago Barcelona raised the stakes again and brought the rest of the team with the front three. Led by Pedro with Messi and David Villa, a midfield three of Xavi, Iniesta and Busquets pushed in behind them. Full-backs Dani Alves and Éric Abidal pushed forward with Javier Mascherano, a centre-half, looking to attack anything that went into the deep-lying striker. I watched Barcelona games for almost two seasons straight and during many of them it was difficult to tell if they had fielded a goalkeeper, such was their dominance of the ball.

But dominance of the ball is one thing, purpose and intent are quite another. Lots of pundits laud Swansea for the way that they have adopted the passing and possession game, but ask anyone who really understands how that style of football is most effective – notably Arsène Wenger – and you will hear talk of a style that, very often, is rudderless when determining the best way to attack teams. Within football Swansea are often criticised for keeping the ball for keeping the ball's sake, whereas at Arsenal and Manchester United under Alex Ferguson, it is clear to see that every attack has a lethal intent to it. Personally, I feel the criticism of Swansea is harsh because I admire any club that chooses to go with the ball-retention approach from scratch, but I do understand where that criticism comes from.

To most of us, ball retention looks the same no matter who the club is, but I'll tell you how you can spot a team that is trying to score and one that is simply keeping the ball and going nowhere. It is all about where the passes are going and Swansea, Arsenal and Barcelona are probably the three best examples of the incremental levels of ball retention, passing and moving and ultimately scoring.

Swansea, as we've discovered, are the only team of the three that play with two wingers, which means that most of their attacks will come from the wide areas. No matter which players start the attacks – the goalkeeper, the ball-playing centre-halves or the deep-lying midfielder – and no matter how they get the ball up the pitch, it always ends up in the wide positions. Swansea can play through teams but it is only to get the ball wide; for the most part they are unable to play through defences. As a result, Swansea very often reach a stalemate in games that see the ball passed from side to side and back again. Yes, they keep the ball, but they become easy to defend against. I have defended against Swansea and once the team gets over the first ten minutes of quick passing and moving, it is actually surprisingly easy to defend against.

At Arsenal, the passing becomes a little more intricate and the team is able to commit more players to attacks who turn up in ever more surprising places. Alex Oxlade-Chamberlain can very often be found roaming along the front line while some moves can see Tomáš Rosický starting wide on the left and ending up receiving a pass that puts him through on goal. Even Jack Wilshere, the so-called orchestrator, will end up exchanging one-twos with Olivier Giroud around the edge of the box. The confidence of the players and their fitness helps them to play in this way.

But the main difference between Swansea and Arsenal is in the way that the ball is moved through the team and played around the opposition box. Arsenal rarely go side to side; they can go straight through teams and they have players who are comfortable collecting the ball with players around them. Their wide players do not stay wide, they drift across the pitch and forward into what we used to call the inside forward positions. We are always taught to remember one thing and one thing only when we play Arsenal: whatever happens, do not follow the ball. Arsenal are a team that plays one-twos all over the pitch but especially around the box.

Top players know when to pass it to one another's feet and when to pass it into space for a player to come on to. They know where each other will move to, they know if the ball coming into them is intended as a one-two or to be held up.

English players, for the most part, have two critical problems in their execution of the game. The first is that they pass the ball straight at a player instead of into the space. This forces the player receiving the ball to control it before he can get his head up, and you would be amazed at how quickly the space closes down in front of an attacking player in the time it takes to control the ball and get his head up.

The second is that players very often dribble the ball towards a teammate before passing it to him from 10 yards away. All this does is drag the defending team straight towards the player receiving the ball and clogs up any space that was free. It is true to say that these bad habits are more common the lower down the league ladder one goes, but there are still plenty of examples of these traits in every Premier League game that you will ever watch.

PLAYING OFFSIDE IS DEAD

With Barcelona having so much of the ball and committing so many players forward in order to keep the ball in advanced positions, opponents had to withdraw all of their players into their own half just to have any chance of holding back the tide. And a curious thing happened: playing offside, as we understand it, all but died out at the Nou Camp.

To be honest, playing offside these days is just too risky. Players are so fast, the passing is crisper and more precise than it has ever been and more importantly, it is quicker. But there is another very good reason for not playing offside; most teams are only playing with one striker and some are playing with none at all. That means that, as a centre-half, there is nobody to take a line off, there is nobody to catch offside. And this is the reason why teams cannot squeeze the pitch against Barcelona and why they always drop off. Any team trying to squeeze the pitch is susceptible to a single pass into the space behind the back four, on to which any one of six players could run.

In the modern game, any team that tries to play offside is routinely caught out. In the 2014 World Cup, Algeria scared the life out of Germany by playing a counter-attacking game that, for some reason, Germany decided to play a high line against. The Germans were extremely fortunate to get away with it. In 2013 Gareth Bale did for Arsenal at White Hart Lane after manager Arsène Wenger had inexplicably employed an offside game against the fastest player in the league.

Even if a team is as good at keeping the ball as Barcelona are, they still can't play a high line against counter-attacking teams. It is football suicide. In the 2014 Copa Del Rey final, Gareth Bale (yes, again) showed exactly why a high line is fraught with danger. Barcelona had possession of the ball but one simple pass down the line found Bale inside his own half, one-on-one with a centre-half who, for reasons known only to himself I'm sure, was holding a line on the halfway line. He should have dropped off 10 or even 20 yards and tried to hold Bale up. Instead, Bale pushed the ball down the line, outpaced Marc Bartra, cut inside and duly scored the winning goal with five minutes to go.

I'm not a massive fan of teams playing a high line but some managers feel that certain games call for it. The key to doing it successfully is to never play a high line if there is no pressure on the ball. It's a basic rule, written on page one of the defensive coaching manual.

But trust me, when I'm on the pitch defending against Manchester City and David Silva has the ball with no pressure on him and Sergio Agüero is about to make a run, it is best for everybody concerned to drop off. It is the safest thing to do. Offside is dead and don't let anybody tell you any different.

THE FALSE NUMBER 9

To this day I still have to put up with people moaning to me that Barcelona don't play with any strikers. I hear it most often when the team are in crossing positions and instead of slinging it into the box they simply come back out and go across the penalty area, looking to work an opening. This is a team that holds the record for the most goals scored in a La Liga season and the most points. Considering they have no out-and-out striker to speak of, I'd say there is little to argue with.

Though most teams in world football could not match Barcelona player for player, they could certainly learn from them, and playing without any recognised striker is perhaps the most obvious example of Barcelona's most recent legacy. The utilisation of players such as Messi, Villa and Pedro as forward-thinking midfielders was given a new name altogether, a name that would help those who needed assistance understanding and adjusting to this new style. It became known as 'the false number 9'.

The false number 9 is a player who is not an out-and-out striker but creates and scores goals. He is generally the player in the most advanced positions. When he drops off, his position is taken by an advancing attacking midfielder. Germany's Thomas Müller is perhaps the best example; he is a wiry, strong, attacking player who operates across the attacking positions for both his club and his country.

Technically he is a fine player, capable of spotting a pass as well as possessing a surprisingly good cross with both feet. But his biggest strength is being what we would call 'a drifter', a player who floats in and out of unorthodox positions, which makes him very awkward for a holding midfielder or a centre-half to pick up. It is his biggest strength because it becomes the team's biggest strength – nobody knows who should pick up so nobody picks him up, and if somebody does manage to tie him down, then the pitch opens up for other players.

If an opposition full-back moves inside the pitch to pressure Müller, then the full-backs will push on outside him to fill the space, and if Müller drops deep then a player like Mario Götze or Mesut Özil will make an inside run off the back of the centre-half. When Müller first broke into the Bayern team he was criticised for not playing like a true striker, but his style has shown us that positions that look unconventional can actually have an order while being supremely effective.

Playing with two number 10s has worked for some of Europe's biggest clubs. Barcelona have done it for years, of course, and Real Madrid have dabbled when Karim Benzema has been unfit. Even Chelsea, thanks to José Mourinho's disdain for Fernando Torres, have played with interchanging forward players instead of recognised strikers.

Thomas Müller is one of the most valuable players that Bayern have, especially when the team can fill the gaps he creates with two advanced full-backs and two electric wingers who both like to come inside the pitch for a shot. Creating space for others is one of the critical factors in successful attacking football and it is also a very difficult trait for fans to spot, which is why players such as Müller are often misunderstood and why it takes us time to warm to them.

IT IS VITAL TO HAVE AN IDENTITY

The most successful football clubs are the ones that have a clear identity, a direction from which they rarely stray. We call it 'a philosophy'. The philosophy is associated particularly with Barcelona's aim to bring players through the La Masia academy and into the first team. At this level, the philosophy is ingrained in the club at every level, but other clubs might base their philosophy purely on which manager is sitting in the hot seat.

There are some well-known phrases in football that, although they have become clichés in interviews, still nonetheless ring true: 'win the battle' is one of them; another is 'go long to come short'; and yet another is 'earn the right to play'. All could be seen during Mourinho's first tenure at Chelsea and when the Blues' talismanic striker, Didier Drogba, was at the peak of his powers. In the first twenty minutes of most matches, Chelsea would sit in, whether they were home or away, and hit the ball long to Drogba – rather unsurprisingly we call this 'getting up the pitch'. Two centre-halves defending this type of ball, especially against a player as physically strong as Drogba, will share the responsibility of defending that first ball.

As one centre-half challenges for the ball, the other drops off to cover his partner in case Drogba wins a flick for a third-man run (generally a player from midfield) or the ball is overhit. Ideally the centre-halves want to come on to the ball while it's in the air rather than allowing themselves to be 'pinned' by Drogba and trying to head it from a standing start. In order to do that they drop off once more, and this time Drogba stands up against them, taking his team 10 yards further up the pitch. When we call players like Drogba a handful, we don't mean it as you might understand it, in terms of being physically strong – any forward can be strong. We mean it in terms of messing with the centre-halves' game, their starting positions, their decision-making and so on. In this case, the centre-halves can't get their starting positions right because Drogba is affecting them, so they simply choose caution, and drop off.

And that has a knock-on effect. The opposition midfield is drawn deeper because they are scared of gaps appearing between their centre-halves and themselves into which a second striker could drop or an attacking midfielder could step. The knock-on effect continues right up the pitch to the strikers who then drop because they don't want to become isolated and detached from the rest of the team.

After twenty minutes the opposition has dropped 15 yards deeper than where they started at the beginning of the game. Once that happens, Chelsea are able to pass the ball around the back with relative freedom and draw players out of spaces that they can then exploit with their superior passing. The whole purpose of these first twenty minutes is to allow the goalkeeper to be able to roll the ball out to his centre-halves with no pressure on them. The team can then start to dominate the game in terms of possession as well as significantly reducing the attacking threat of the opposition. So winning the battle is not about chasing round like a madman trying to injure opposition players; it refers to winning the tactical exchange at the start of the game by sticking to the orders of the manager, in this case by 'going long to come short'. Don't let anybody tell you that there is no place for the long ball in today's game because if it is used with an ideology in mind it can be fundamental to earning 'the right to play'.

Identity is a huge part of football. Some teams can exert their philosophy better than others because they have better players, but every single team has an identity nonetheless.

Last season my footballing friends who are in a position to talk down to me when it comes to tactics, such is their knowledge and experience, all cited one team as the standout example of a club that nailed its identity with one signing. Stoke City had as strong an identity as any club in the Premier League under former manager Tony Pulis; it wasn't always pretty but the long-ball approach combined with the long throws of Rory Delap worked very well for them. When Pulis left the club, Mark Hughes took over and set about reshaping the team and the style of play. Unfortunately for Hughes, he didn't have the players that he wanted and by January the club was hovering dangerously close to the relegation places, just four points off the bottom three.

Hughes needed pace in order to play an effective 4–2–3–1 system. Marko Arnautović, the supremely talented (Austrian) midfielder, was suffering as a result of his side not being able to get up the pitch and support himself and Peter Crouch. Then, in a masterstroke, Hughes signed Peter

10

The ten best players of the last twenty years

Lionel Messi
Zinedine Zidane
Cristiano Ronaldo
Xavi Hernández
Ronaldinho
Paul Scholes
Paolo Maldini
Thierry Henry
Ryan Giggs
Andrés Iniesta

Odemwingie from Cardiff as part of a swap deal that saw Kenwyne Jones go the other way, and on that signing the fortunes of the club turned.

Odemwingie's signing is a great example of one or two adages. Firstly, that certain attributes such as pace are key to certain formations; and secondly, that there is some truth behind any manager's claim that they need time to build a team. A manager won't always be able to sign the players he wants when he takes a new job; transfer windows are a factor for a start, but very often the right players simply aren't for sale and the manager is forced to bide his time. Believe me, it is very easy to fill up a squad with the wrong players and sign players for the sake of it. Arsène Wenger constantly uses the phrase 'the right quality' when talking to the press about signing players. In other words, 'We won't sign any old player just so that you have something to write about.'

Before it was brought to my attention I hadn't considered Peter Odemwingie to be the signing of last season, but that is exactly what many aficionados in the game believe. The impact of Odemwingie's arrival on the upturn in fortunes of Stoke City in the 2013–14 season is significant. From January, Stoke were able to play further up the pitch and, as a result, the form of Peter Crouch improved dramatically. With teammates now closer to Crouch, players like Arnautović were able to perform their creative trickery in the right parts of the pitch while left-winger Oussama Assaidi, on loan from Liverpool, became a revelation during the run-in. Odemwingie's signing brought pace to Hughes' team and balance to his formation as well as giving new-found form and confidence to his teammates. He was never going to win any awards but, then again, the people who tend to dish them out don't really know what they're watching.

Successful teams have an identity; I could tell you exactly what the identity of every team in the Premier League was last season, or at least, what they were trying to do in that respect. Swansea and Southampton both have attractive styles of football, which is part of their identity ingrained in their respective philosophies. Crystal Palace were really struggling to implement their identity until Tony Pulis arrived. West Ham are another team that have a clear identity – it isn't pretty but it works for them, just. They play balls into Andy Carroll and ask players to get around him for the knock-downs, and if you wanted to know why their manager Sam Allardyce persists with Kevin Nolan, the answer is simple – it's because Big Sam is a stats man at heart and Nolan consistently has the highest number of touches in the penalty box compared to any other player.

The importance of having an identity – and moreover one that everybody buys into – is vital to every club in world football.

But teams struggling with their identity, struggle, in turn, to achieve what they should be achieving on the pitch. Step forward Tottenham and, in particular, Manchester United.

In truth, the problems at Manchester United began before David Moyes took the job, thanks to a chronic lack of investment in the playing squad by Sir Alex Ferguson. Like Arnautović at Stoke, Juan Mata is a player who needs pace and movement around him. What he doesn't need is a player like Marouane Fellaini. Who was played as a defensive midfielder, which he isn't.

Consider this: in the 2013–14 season, Manchester United fielded fifty-two different line-ups with no two the same from one game to the next, and they played fifty-two games. If that isn't an identity crisis then I don't know what is. The identity of the club under Sir Alex Ferguson was such that Manchester United didn't change for anyone; his players were continually being told that they were the best. One player who used to play for United told me, 'Park Ji-sung was a prime example – the boss used to tell him before every big game that nobody could live with him, nobody could get near him, he was the best. We knew he wasn't, but he believed it and he'd go out on the pitch and destroy teams.'

The juxtaposition between the mind-set of what was largely the same group of players under Ferguson and Moyes is stark. Before the Liverpool game at Old Trafford David Moyes said, 'Their league position suggests that they are ahead of us and they possibly do come here as favorites,' and after the Manchester City game which United lost 3–0 at Old Trafford Moyes was quoted as saying, 'We have played a very good side playing at the sort of level we are aspiring to.' Let my friend tell you how those comments went down with the players: 'We would never have heard anything like that from Sir Alex, absolutely never; we were always the best and if we weren't then it was never our fault. For the first time, the players were being told that they were inferior to other teams, it wasn't a happy time for anyone.'

Moyes changed the identity of the club and Manchester United went from a team that had the confidence to attack teams home and away to a team that were set up not to lose. It is no surprise that United had the best away record in the Premier League, where they were defensively strong and picked teams off who were under pressure as the home side to attack. But at Old Trafford it was a different story, with no pace and no idea of how to attack teams when the onus was on them to do so. As a result, United were picked off time and again by counterattacking teams.

COACHING

Managers are hindering their successors
(understandably)

Most managers have a tendency to cut off their nose to spite their face. I have been playing football at every level for almost fifteen years and almost every manager I've played under worries about one thing: is the oldest player in the squad going to take my job? Talented older players are routinely paid off for no other reason than the manager wants to remove any possibility of an in-house coup d'état, particularly if that player is showing signs of wanting to stay in the game after he hangs up his boots. The dressing-room voice that was so appreciated a couple of years previously is now a warning sign. It is almost as if a paranoia alarm has suddenly gone off in the manager's head and, as a result, measures are taken. Believe me, the amount of potential coaching and managerial talent that is kicked out the door in football is a disgrace.

Once again, the Continent has shown us what we should have been doing with players who want to stay in the game. At Barcelona, former players were fed back into the club's coaching system: Tito Vilanova, Pep Guardiola and current Barcelona manager Luis Enrique all began their managerial careers with Barcelona B, and the current manager of Barcelona B, Eusebio Sacristán, played for Barcelona for seven years between 1988 and 1995. A shared philosophy with evolving ideas leads to a dynasty.

But Manchester United, at least, have taken the bait. Despite the fact that Ryan Giggs had a fairly shaky time as United manager at the end of the 2013–14 season, the club has retained him as assistant manager to Louis van Gaal. The club has also at one time or another given coaching roles to former players Phil Neville, Nicky Butt and Paul Scholes, with varying degrees of success. The point is, they have already bought into the Manchester United way, they understand the club, they have been successful and want the club to continue to be successful and, above all, they know what it takes to win football matches at that club because they understand what is expected from the fans and how it needs to be delivered. Why on earth would any club, at any level, throw away that kind of dedication? And yet, amazingly, they do. Most of the time it is because the structure of the club is not right and too many decisions are left to the manager when they should be taken in the boardroom.

The first thing that any club should do the moment it hears of one of its more successful ex-players falling out of football is to get on the phone and ask whether he wants to stay in the game or not. Any player who is held in high regard at one particular club has a value, and chief executives all over the country should be saying to them, 'You know how we do things, you are respected and understand our philosophy, would you consider taking a role with us?' And yes, since you ask, I'm talking about myself, albeit on behalf of all those other players in the same boat.

COACHING DOES NOT EXIST

Here is the thing that you probably didn't realise about football. When you are a professional player, the coaching that you've had in the academy largely stops. Save for the odd disguised ball session in pre-season, which is really a fitness session, coaching does not exist in the way that you probably think it does. Few clubs, certainly in the Premier League, will introduce a session to work on technique.

Don't get me wrong, technique will be a by-product of sessions such as crossing and finishing or keep-ball, but these sessions have a primary purpose depending, almost exclusively, on what opposition you are playing at the weekend. If we are playing Arsenal, Chelsea or Manchester City, we will work on keeping our shape by playing six attacking players against our midfield four and our back four so our defensive mind-set is sharp. But if we're playing a team close to the bottom of the league and we fancy our chances, then we'll work on sessions that take the game to them, such as winning the ball back and overloads of play.

What I'm about to say isn't true of every club and certainly at the biggest clubs there are coaches for the coaches, such is the level of the budget. Many clubs don't have that depth of luxury, of course, but even so, they don't help themselves. The root cause of the problem with coaching at many clubs is that you have guys who were born, raised and now live in certain parts of the country and have no desire to rock the boat and say how things are, no matter which owner is in place. They are Mr Middlesbrough or Mr Leeds or wherever; they want to stay living in the area and do not want to move again; they have kids and mortgages to pay. They do the bare minimum to be seen and heard. They come in, sit on the fence, never raise their voice and try to stay that way for as long as possible. No extra training for the kids, no advice, nothing that alerts anybody to their existence. In fact, they do nothing other than suck up to the manager and certain senior players who they believe have enough influence to have their back if things get choppy. It is a cancer in our game and it needs to stop.

And it isn't fair on the kids who come through to the first team because at many of the clubs that fit the description above, the technical coaching afforded to them generally ceases on the day they sign their first professional contract. Kids are expected to be ready to go on the day they sign that deal, but you and I both know that, in football, players never stop learning. The best kids will try to improve themselves but very often their attempt to improve their technique is misguided and they work on things that simply don't need working on. I actually find it quite hard to watch them and have, at certain moments, taken it upon myself to put sessions on for them at the end of training based on what I think they should be trying to improve. And, all the while, the coaches who should be taking the session stare at me through the window of their nice warm office.

At every club I have ever been at, all I can ever hear coming from the academy training pitch are shouts of 'quicker, quicker', and when I glance over I see the centre-half or the holding midfielder bringing the ball out of defence. Very often the opposition have dropped off, including the strikers, meaning that the players should be learning about sucking players out of position. But instead the message being drilled into them is that everything has to be done at top speed – yet when they make a mistake the coach shouts, 'Relax on the ball!' The conflict in the information that these kids receive is so alarming that it's a wonder we produce any players at all.

And it is this early stage that has an effect on the big picture. Let me pick a taboo subject that encapsulates what I'm talking about. In the game we call it being 'streetwise' but it also goes by the names 'know-how' and 'game management'. It is the part of the game that in England we like to pretend we're above, but in reality, deep down, we know it is costing us matches. At the centre of this part of the game is diving. I'm not necessarily talking about throwing yourself to the ground to win a penalty when nobody is near; I'm talking about buying fouls all over the pitch in order to manage the game.

Consider the comments made by England coach Gary Neville, after West Ham were beaten at the Emirates Stadium by Arsenal in the 2013–14 season. When Matt Jarvis was clipped in the box by Bacary Sagna, he didn't go to ground but stayed on his feet. If he had gone down West Ham would have been given a penalty; instead, they got nothing. Neville said after the game, 'We are the only country that thinks the way that we do about diving.

Every single country in Europe, in the world, would have said, "He is mad." We actually think, "Fantastic. Well done, son. You've stayed on your feet." We are the only country that thinks like that. And you can say, "It's great for us. That's how we've been brought up," but when you've been through the professional game and you've been stitched up by foreign players so many times playing in European competitions as a kid, through European competitions – we're going to have to join it.'

That may be hard for you to hear but it's true and it isn't confined to penalties, but fouls all over the pitch. Cesc Fàbregas was a master at winning fouls; when I had Cesc cornered or facing his own goal, he'd simply fall to his knees and the referee always gave him a free-kick. Certainly, if you are clipped in the box, there is no reward for staying on your feet, but the rewards for going down are enormous and, in the context of the game as a whole, all of those marginal gains add up to something significant. They can determine the outcome of a game, I've seen it so many times.

Nobody is talking about cheating, it is more about having the wherewithal to realise that when you are in a tricky situation on the pitch and you feel a hand on your back or shoulder, it may be prudent to hit the deck. After all, referees cannot tell how much pressure a player is exerting when they place their hands on the body of an opponent. I learned that from Cristiano Ronaldo who, whenever I put my hand on his shoulder with literally no pressure whatsoever, would always hit the deck as if somebody had him on the end of a fishing line and had suddenly reeled him in very quickly. He always got the foul, even though I can assure you I never fouled him once.

So many people ask me if, as professional footballers, we practise diving. I mean, I ask you. How do you practise a dive? It's quite ridiculous. So when you're standing in the pub watching the TV and a young English kid goes racing through on goal in the last minute of the World Cup final and takes it round the keeper but has his legs clipped, and the ball is running out of play, what would you shout? I'll tell you what I'd shout: 'Go down.'

GOALKEEPERS CAN PLAY THE SWEEPER ROLE

It is true to say that the influence of the World Cup is far and wide, from the kids who are inspired to ask their parents for their first football, to the ardent fans who watch in their millions, to professionals like us looking to pick up anything new that the top players might be doing.

And out of the World Cup in 2014 came a game changer. The emergence at the finals of German goalkeeper Manuel Neuer as a keeper-cum-sweeper was both an interesting spectacle and a bad day for less confident goalkeepers all over Europe. If there is one thing that I know, and one thing that I've explained earlier in this book, fashion trends in football affect everybody and Neuer's exceptional trait for racing off his line and snuffing out attacks with two decent feet was something that I saw coveted from our own goalkeeping coach on the training ground in only our first week back from the pre-season break. I remarked to a teammate that the season ahead would be full of goalkeeping errors, as they all tried to replicate the best in the business in Neuer.

Any goalkeeper can spring from his line to head the ball away, though Neuer's brilliance was that very often he'd control the ball and make a pass that got Germany playing again. In fact, he made a lot of passes. From the first game to the last, Neuer made a total of 244 passes. For the record, Lionel Messi made 242. While it's true that Messi is a dribbler it is still a phenomenal statistic, especially as both teams made the final in Rio. But while Neuer may well be the best exponent of the keeper-cum-sweeper role and rightly won a huge amount of plaudits, he certainly isn't an innovator.

When Stoke City travelled to Old Trafford to face Manchester United in 2008, their game plan was a typically stubborn defensive style that looked to exploit set pieces. They did this primarily through Rory Delap's long throws, which he would hurl into the opposition box at lightning speed towards several teammates, who would run in and launch themselves towards the ball hoping to get a slight touch and take the ball towards the goal. But United had recognised the threat of Stoke, and in particular the fact that they defended deep and relied on long balls to their striker who would try to win a foul or a throw.

To counter the threat, United squeezed the pitch and played Edwin van der Sar as a sweeper. Stoke continually played the ball down the sides of the United back four where the hope was that their centre-half pairing of Vidić and Evans would take the easy option and play the ball out for a Stoke throw. What they actually did was play the ball to Van der Sar, who was playing in the sweeper position, and he would transfer the ball out to the other side. Two things happened: United were able to recycle Stoke's attacks into attacks of their own by transferring the ball to the other side of the pitch so quickly that Stoke couldn't squeeze up the pitch, and Stoke didn't win a single throw-in anywhere near the United goal. United won the match at a canter, 5–0.

The 'fashion' of playing a goalkeeper as a sweeper will now take over and every manager who tries to play a passing brand of football will encourage their goalkeeper to become an outfield player at certain moments of the game. And my prediction is that a fair amount of mistakes will ensue as goalkeepers of all standards try to act out their manager's new-found expectations of what exactly a goalkeeper is expected to do.

TACKLING IS A WEAKNESS

I make no apologies for repeating myself from previous columns and even my first book, because what Spain's Xabi Alonso said about tackling is perhaps one of the most brilliant and fundamental pieces of footballing gospel that any player has ever uttered in the history of the game. Alonso was interviewed by the *Guardian* when he happened to pass comment on the fact that so many academy players at Liverpool, when quizzed about their biggest strength in the back pages of match-day programmes, would give the answer 'tackling'.

'I can't get into my head that football development would educate tackling as a quality, something to learn, to teach, a characteristic of your play,' said Alonso. 'How can that be a way of seeing the game? I just don't understand football in those terms. Tackling is a [last] resort and you will need it, but it isn't a quality to aspire to, a definition.'

One year earlier I had made the same claim in the changing room of the club that I was playing for at the time. I was absolutely laughed out of the room. Nobody believed that I was talking any sense whatsoever; in fact, they told me that I was tactically naïve.

When the game is played in the same way for years and years, as it has been in England particularly, it is difficult for some people, even players, to see the wood for the trees. To me it was obvious that tackling for the sake of tackling was a real flaw in English football. Even if you won the ball it would spin off in any direction and if it went to an opposition player then you were left on the floor and out of the game. With the game played as fast as modern football is these days, that is a huge gamble – actually, it is tactically naïve.

SO HOW DOES A TEAM WIN THE BALL BACK IF IT DOESN'T TACKLE?

In the 2014 World Cup, the teams that were defensive didn't tackle; they stood up and asked their opposite number to take them on and get past them, and as a result the best exponents, such as Chile and Honduras, took better teams – which, on paper, should have wiped the floor with them – to penalty shootouts.

This is probably the most important piece of advice in the book. In fact, if you only take one thing from this book then let it be this: there are two main ways of winning the ball back in modern football – press the opposition until they make a mistake, or wait for the opposition to misplace a pass or overhit a cross when they attack. The two are distinguished by whether or not a team is an attacking, pressing side or a defensive, organised side. But they both have a fundamental similarity in that they do not involve tackling on the ground.

In 2001, Sir Alex Ferguson, a manager with a fierce reputation for dispensing with players he felt were no longer at their best or were becoming bigger than the sum of the team, sold his best central defender, Jaap Stam, for £15.3 million to Lazio. Many pundits attributed the surprise decision to an autobiography in which Stam had been less than flattering about some of his teammates. The reality was very different.

Ferguson had been told by United's analysis department that Stam was making fewer tackles in a match and he concluded, wrongly, that the Dutchman was past his best. Nothing could have been further from the truth. Jaap Stam was in fact at the peak of his powers – he was very quick, he was strong and, above all, he was hardly ever out of position, all of which meant he very rarely *needed* to make a tackle. Stam would go on to win the Coppa Italia with Lazio, the Supercoppa Italiana with AC Milan, as well as reaching a second Champions League final in 2005. Of his decision to sell Stam to Lazio, Sir Alex Ferguson would later say, 'When I think of disappointments, obviously Jaap Stam was always a disappointment to me, I made a bad decision there.'

If you were to ask any striker in world football if Jaap Stam had given them an easy ride in the match, every single one of them would have said 'no'. But tackling is a trait that is so easy for a crowd and statisticians to buy into; after all, it shows passion, doesn't it? It shows commitment and honesty as well as desire and leadership. Doesn't it? No. What it actually shows is a player making up for his shortcomings as both a technician and an athlete.

As footballers, we can tell when players are playing to the crowd. We know exactly when that is happening and the rest of us hate it, even if the player is on our own team – in fact, *especially* if the player is on our own team. Players who throw themselves around do so for your adoration; it is the easiest way in the world to get a cheer from the crowd and release a few endorphins. What is harder is to play a killer through-ball in an attempt to win the game, knowing full well that if it's cut out the crowd will more than likely let out a collective groan.

Sliding tackles, which are more like blocks now anyway, are becoming rarer and should be reserved for those moments that require last-ditch defending, such as when Javier Mascherano brilliantly blocked Holland's Arjen Robben as the Dutchman was about to shoot during the dying moments of their semi-final in Brazil. After the game Mascherano revealed in an interview that he'd actually torn his anus making that block, and if that isn't a reason to stay on your feet, I don't know what is.

THANKFULLY, 50–50 TACKLES ARE DYING OUT

Watch how many times English players go in for a 50–50 header with each other with no clue as to where the ball will end up. They do it purely for bravado and to show the fans that they're trying. Players in England just want to win the header and if they do they think their job has been done. Elsewhere, players are trying to pass to each other when they head the ball. Winning the header for the sake of it is a coward's way to play football: it does not take responsibility for the ball in any way and the turnover of possession is high. Pep Guardiola's great Barcelona side never got the credit they deserved for heading balls that were dropping out of the air to the feet of their teammates. A ball dropping out of the air on to your head is still an opportunity to pass the ball and build an attack, and should not be viewed as an opportunity to clean somebody out and make yourself look good in the process, as it is in the Premier League.

The number of youth team midfielders I see run straight through the back of an opposition player as the ball drops out of the sky is ridiculous. The correct thing to do is to get your body into the player, put your arm over his shoulder – it won't be a foul – and head the ball to a teammate whom you have identified while the ball is in the air. It doesn't look as spectacular, it doesn't look as if you're trying as hard as you ought to be, it may give the impression that you are scared of a 50–50 challenge and it might not get a big cheer from the crowd, who want to see somebody have their head taken off – but, trust me, it is absolutely the right thing to do in order to retain possession, and footballers and people who understand football will appreciate it.

If I'm a manager, then I don't want my midfielder to clean somebody out and head the ball straight back to the opposition goalkeeper in the process. What good is that to me, what have we gained? I want him to head the ball to a teammate because three things happen as a result of my team having the ball: the opposition can't score, we can keep the ball moving between us and tire the opposition out as they chase it, and once that happens we have a better chance of picking them off and scoring a goal.

The top three worst shouts that you will hear from inept academy coaches on the training pitch and the rebuffs from the world's best players

☺ **'Space doesn't score goals; players do, so mark the player!'**

Response: *'Look for spaces. All day. I'm always looking. All day, all day. Here? No. There? No. People who haven't played don't always realise how hard that is. Space, space, space. It's like being on the PlayStation. I think damn, the defender's here, play it there. I see the space and pass. That's what I do.'*
Xavi Hernández

Verdict: Space wins football matches. Condensing the space is the key to stopping the opposition. A prime example of this can be seen in the Costa Rica v Holland match in the World Cup quarter-final in Brazil. Holland simply could not break Costa Rica down, such was the tightness of their back five and the screening of the midfield four. Danny Murphy, the pundit for the game, said that he was surprised that Holland had not changed formations; it wouldn't have made any difference because, regardless of where the Dutch positioned their players on the pitch, the space remained condensed. Costa Rica didn't mark the Dutch players – instead, they condensed the space and ended up taking the match to penalties. As the legendary Ernst Happel, coach of the 1978 Dutch total football side, once said: 'If you mark man-to-man, you're sending out eleven donkeys.'

☺ 'Make him control it! Pass to feet!'

Response: *'Playing simply is the hardest thing there is. The art is to play the ball so that the receiver has the overview of the pitch and can go to action effectively. The speed with which that happens is the difference between a good and a bad player.'* Johan Cruyff

Verdict: In some cases passing the ball to feet is obvious – a centre-half to a holding midfield player, for example, so that he can bounce it back again. But in more attacking areas of the pitch, especially the wide areas, the ball needs to be passed into the space so that players can step on to the ball, and it is this that Cruyff is referring to. Taking unnecessary touches slows the game down, it forces the ball back and ultimately it makes a good player look bad. My grievance with young English wingers is that their mind-set is one of getting the ball to their feet, making sure it is exactly where they want it, before they set off at full tilt while looking down at the ball. They seem to have their feet glued to the touchline until the ball comes to them. When Cruyff talks about an overview of the pitch, he is referring to somebody playing the ball into the space for a player to step on to, so that the game is rhythmic, it is fluid, and he doesn't need to look down. If you're looking down at the ball how can you see players making angles and runs for you?

☺ **'Do your skill in the final third – it doesn't matter if you lose it there!'**

Response: *'In the playground I always played against bigger kids and I always wanted the ball. Without the ball, I feel lost.'* Andrés Iniesta

Verdict: Players will lose possession of the ball – it is an occupational hazard, especially amongst those of us who are brave on the ball and try to make things happen and don't mind the crowd getting on our backs for giving the ball away when trying to create a chance for another. And on that note, fans should always try to recognise when a player is attempting to make something happen and refrain from jeering at him if he gives it away. After all, the game is about scoring goals, and a team can't do that if it doesn't have players who are prepared to accept that they will sometimes have their through-ball cut out. The problem is that the academies do not explain themselves very well. While it is commendable to persuade a kid to express himself, what he actually hears is, 'Do what you want and if you lose the ball, it doesn't matter.'

At one Premier League academy I visited, a very enthusiastic coach told me that all the players have individual targets during matches – the winger, for example, had been tasked with delivering at least twenty crosses, ten per half. And as I watched him I saw exactly what I would expect to see from a kid who has been asked to hit a specific number. He was crossing the ball from everywhere, instead of keeping it and passing the ball back across the pitch so that the attack could continue from a

10 The ten best players of the future playing now

Ross Barkley, Everton

Raphaël Varane, Real Madrid

Julian Draxler, Schalke 04

David Alaba, Bayern Munich

Luke Shaw, Manchester United

Raheem Sterling, Liverpool

Gerard Deulofeu, Barcelona

Adnan Januzaj, Manchester United

Romelu Lukaku, Everton

James Rodríguez, Real Madrid

different direction. He tried to cross it from 10 yards inside the opposition half at one point.

Twenty crosses per game! That sort of coaching is so misguided. The kid comes off the pitch thinking he has played well because he achieved his target. The striker has ten shots instead of passing the ball to create better chances on at least eight occasions. And what happens? The team become nothing more than individuals – they become England, full of players running in straight lines, dribbling the ball towards each other, giving the ball away after six or seven passes because they panic and are unsure of how to get the ball into the positions of the pitch that affect the outcome of a football match. Incidentally, you can tell an average team by the six-pass rule, which says a team that are pressed and not comfortable passing the ball around will concede possession on the sixth pass.

And that brings us on to passing, something so simple that it's almost impossible for a lot of players to get right. Don't get me wrong, every coach that I've ever worked with will shout 'take care' if a pass is a little wayward of its intended target, but the most important thing when passing the ball is that, wherever possible, keep the bloody thing on the floor. The moment the ball leaves the ground, even by half a dozen inches, everything becomes more difficult and takes twice as long. Entire attacks can be killed by one pass that leaves the floor because the player has to control it and move it out of his feet.

Football in England faces challenges at every level and it is right to suggest that if there are problems at the top, then it's very likely that there will be problems right the way down. How many times do you hear about or read an interview with somebody from the FA who says something like, 'We went to Germany/Spain for six weeks to see how they do things and we took away some fantastic ideas'? Therein lies a critical problem with the way England approach football.

When the German team really began to show the world how to play modern football with fantastic Dortmund and Bayern Munich teams, and as a result the national team, members of the FA's coaching team decamped to Germany to learn the secrets. It was exactly the same before that with Spain and before that, Brazil.

Replication will only ever succeed in producing a side slightly worse than that which it is modelled on, because it will be twenty years after the original. Twenty years to bring the players through in the new style, by which time the nations at the forefront of modern football, like Brazil, Spain and Germany, have innovated and produced a new style. England have been playing catch-up football for sixty years. My guess is that you will see an England team trying to play like Germany in about twenty years' time, and while you're watching that, Germany, Spain, Brazil or another innovative nation will be hoisting trophies above their heads for us to look at on the back pages of the same newspapers with the same damning headlines that we have now.

WHATEVER HAPPENS, NEVER, EVER GIVE UP

Eight years ago I watched a reserve match with a scout who used to look me up when he was in the area. He used to appreciate my input towards players he was interested in, as he'd been retired from playing the game for a long time and liked to have a current player alongside him where possible to point out anything that he might miss. I asked him who we were focusing on and he said, 'City have got a kid up front that everyone is raving about – quick, good feet and scores goals. The cat's out of the bag but I just want to see what the fuss is about.'

He wasn't the only scout looking at a kid who must have been fifteen or sixteen at the time. Half of Chelsea's staff seemed to be sitting around us in a stand that was otherwise devoid of any paying spectators. In the middle of them was Stuart Pearce, the Manchester City and (somehow) the England Under-21 manager.

The game started and I watched with a sense of anticipation. Frankly, in the first half the boy struggled. He looked awful if I'm honest, but then his team weren't playing that well. Even so, I was not impressed and was seriously thinking about going home.

In the second half he scored a hat trick and a week later he made his full Premier League debut. In fact, in that same season he became the only player ever to score in the FA Youth Cup, the FA Cup and the Premier League. In June 2014, Daniel Sturridge scored England's first goal of the World Cup against Italy after a season in which he'd scored twenty-one league goals for Liverpool.

The point of all this is that it pays to stay. You would be horrified by the number of scouts who think they can do their job in the first five minutes of a game before jumping in the car and heading home. I wasn't spotted until my twenties, and many of my friends, better players than I ever was, were never spotted. The waste of talent in this country is frightening.

And it isn't confined to young kids. The most talented players in the game aren't immune to the dreaded trapdoor, even when they appear to be at the height of their powers; the difference is that the reasons are nearly always political rather than being down to a bad decision. Dimitar Berbatov is widely regarded as one of the most skilful players to have played in the Premier League; certainly he was a player that I was very fond of watching. And what you probably won't be surprised to hear either is that when he signed for Fulham, his presence created a couple of problems for the club that they hadn't really had before.

A friend of mine who works for Fulham told me: 'We had a really good, tight-knit squad at Fulham just before he came in; the lads knew each other well and had a good level of confidence. Even so, when he signed for us, we were really excited – he was the bit of nous that we needed in our team and the lads were really excited about working with him. The problem was that from day one he didn't really interact with anybody and some of the players he didn't talk to at all. It was almost as if he felt that by coming from United, Fulham were beneath him and, by extension, the players were beneath him.

'So the manager called all the staff together and said, "Look, we need to sort this out before it gets out of hand and the atmosphere goes completely, does anybody have any suggestions?"

'So I spoke up and said that I was very close to a coach at United and I could simply call him up and see how they'd handled him at United. The manager liked that idea and so the next day I called the coach at United and told him what was going on with Berba.

'I said to him, "He's creating a bit of friction, he doesn't talk to any of the players except on the pitch when he's berating them in front of the cameras for not passing him the ball. We explained to him that he would have to run a channel or two every now and again because we can't always pass the ball into his feet, and he just looked at us in disgust. The team spirit is becoming fragile and the other players are losing confidence because they think they're not good enough. You've got to help us, mate, how did you deal with it at United?"

'There was a bit of a silence before he replied, almost as

if he couldn't believe that I'd asked him the question in the first place. "How did we deal with it?" he asked. "Well, it's simple really, mate – we fucked him off to Fulham. Good luck."'

Sometimes there really are no friends in football.

MESSI v RONALDO

I don't like these debates generally but this is a question that I am asked more than any other and everyone has their favourite so I may as well offer an opinion. The truth is, both Ronaldo and Messi are world-class players, fantastic to watch, integral to their respective clubs, invaluable commercially and fiercely competitive.

The first thing to say about both players is that their sheer hunger should inspire anyone who wants to play football or appreciates genuine commitment to the cause. As I've said, hunger doesn't come from trying to take somebody's legs off with a ridiculous 'tackle'. Hunger comes from wanting the ball; it comes from wanting to show everyone how good you are, not how tough you think you are.

I can always tell how hungry and how confident any kid in any academy is by something so innocuous that most of us probably just accept it as part of the game. It is something that a scout once told me, a man who has plucked some of the biggest names in world football out of obscurity. The next time you watch a football match, wait for the moment when the ball is rolling off the pitch at a snail's pace and an attacking player is jogging behind it with no pressure on him. He has already accepted the throw-in before the ball has gone out. We call this trait 'passing responsibility' and we usually attach it to players who pass to teammates in worse positions than themselves because they are uncomfortable on the ball. In both cases, it is a real blight on the quality of the game.

Watch what happens when the very best players like Ronaldo and Messi are faced with the same scenario. They have so much confidence in themselves and so much hunger to get to the ball that they sprint after it to keep it in play, because they know that they can turn and attack the full-back who is labouring after them. As a manager or even a scout, I don't want players who are content to let the ball roll out for a throw-in; I want a player who can't wait to get to the ball so that he can turn and take an opponent on. The lack of respect that some of the kids coming through in the game have for the ball is a disgrace and the way that some coaches simply accept it is even worse. This little trait will tell you everything you need to know about a player – this innocent little nuance will separate the very best from the rest; it will showcase confidence and ability once the ball is retrieved and it all comes from the hunger to keep the ball in play.

But the real fun comes once these two players have the ball at their feet and this is also where we can see the first real differences between the pair. Ronaldo doesn't go past players like Messi – very few players in the world can do what Messi does. In fact, at the level that Messi operates, nobody can do what Messi does. But if you want to know why speed is essential in today's game, look at Ronaldo and Bale, who push the ball past players and then run past them in straight lines. In a flat race nobody will catch them.

Messi, however, runs at players at full speed while keeping the ball under close control, and not in a straight line but in every direction. Trust me, there's a huge difference between the two in this respect. It means that Messi can dribble past players in any part of the pitch and not just at the retreating defence, which is generally when Ronaldo is in full flight. No player I've ever seen can do what Lionel Messi can do, and that includes Ronaldo, whereas the players who can do what Ronaldo can do? Well, you don't have to go far: Real Madrid have another one on the other wing.

During the 2014 World Cup Neil Lennon said, 'I think there's a subconscious affection for Messi that maybe isn't there for Ronaldo because Messi is just a pure footballer, whereas there's a theory that Ronaldo is a little bit more manufactured. Messi is very unassuming.' I can totally understand what Lennon is saying. I look at Ronaldo and see a player who has been coached to near-perfection, I see a player who has been told to keep improving his strengths by working on the quickness of his feet with ladder training, and his physique with a carefully planned weights programme. When I look at Ronaldo, I see a perfect Nike advert, one of those YouTube videos designed to motivate everybody who watches it with clips of him wearing a parachute while doing sprint drills and lifting weights in the gym.

When I look at Lionel Messi, however, I see a player who has been told to go on the pitch and do whatever he wants because that will win his team the game. Players like Messi are the exception to the rule; they are, in the main, uncoachable. Don't get me wrong, they work harder than anybody else in training but that is almost a by-product of the way they play the game.

Almost everything that Messi does is off the cuff, and that is why I will never understand the question of which player is the best in the world. Ronaldo may have had a better season than Messi in 2013–14 but that doesn't make him a better player than Messi, I'm afraid. There is no question in my mind, Lionel Messi is the greatest player of all time. There is no doubt about it, and I don't need four Ballons d'Or to tell me that, I just need my eyes. I know what I'm looking at and I know the difference between a pure player and a manufactured player. Ronaldo is the example of how good a player can be when an athlete is plucked off the street and trained to within an inch of his life. Messi is an example of a player who is pure football and I personally get a huge amount of enjoyment from the unknown element that embodies his game.

Cristiano Ronaldo once said that God put him on this planet to play football. We'll have to ask Lionel Messi if he remembers doing that.

EPILOGUE

'You'll see it's all a show, keep 'em laughing as you go, just remember that the last laugh is on you'

Life of Brian

Be careful about the people you give it the big one to. It seems to me that lots of kids these days want to give it the big one because their idols give it the big one. Instagram is rammed full of show-offs such as Floyd Mayweather, a boxer who posted a short video of two women, bored in his bedroom while he polished his collection of watches – so he gave them two huge wads of cash each and devised a competition to see who could count to $100,000 the fastest. Unfortunately, this is all the kids see. In my experience many, not all, of the kids at top-level Premiership teams want to start earning big money quickly for two reasons. Firstly, so that they can tell everybody that they have a lot of money and, secondly, so that they can show everybody that they have a lot of money. But every now and again they can pick on the wrong person.

All this is bullshit, it means nothing. Not to me, anyway. There is nothing like seeing the best players in the game, there is nothing more exciting than just watching football the way it should be played, and I've seen them all. I saw Gabriel Batistuta rip defences to pieces with nothing more than the spread of fear amongst the opposition back four. I saw Glenn Hoddle and, later, Paul Gascoigne prove that an entire football nation did not know what to do with skill and finesse – and that was only twenty years ago.

I told two clubs to sign Luka Modrić before he went to Spurs – neither of them listened. When I played against him I was forced to tell Modrić that he was the finest midfielder I'd seen at White Hart Lane since Gazza himself. I sent a DVD of his performance against us to one of the managers and received a text back saying, 'OK, you were right, try getting twenty-five right.'

I nutmegged Real Madrid's Álvaro Arbeloa; I told Edwin van der Sar to pick the ball out of the net so we could restart the game. I've played against the finest players in the world who have won the Champions League. I eased Ronaldo off the ball, I was put in the stand by Mascherano; I picked Wayne Rooney off the floor when he'd fallen on his arse. I asked Xabi Alonso, after he hit yet another long pass over the head of World Cup winner Fernando Torres, if he had anything else in his armoury.

And speaking of World Cup winners, I cleaned out Juan Mata on the left wing, I shook hands with Pepe Reina after a wonder save in a match that my team played against him, but I also kicked Ashley Cole so that he screamed like a little girl. I hugged David Luiz when I swapped shirts with him. I told Nemanja Vidić that I'd clean my car with his shirt if he promised to do the same with mine. I swapped shirts with Rio Ferdinand because my friend had asked me to get a shirt with the gold Premier League Championship badges on it.

The moral is, be careful about how and who you give it the big one to. Done well, it can be funny; done badly, you can lose a lot more than your shirt.

I've seen players show off all over the world. I saw it in Marbella when a Sunderland player ordered a €75,000 bottle of champagne just because a youth team player was wandering around with two regular-sized bottles, with his hat on back to front, giving it the big one and pouring champagne into the mouth of any girl who wanted it. When it came, the €75,000 bottle was waist-height and had to be brought out by two waiters using a pulley. That pissed on the youth team player's parade very quickly indeed.

But it's in Las Vegas where anybody can trip up – even those players who have millions in the bank can be dwarfed. On a recent visit, we booked into the Wynn, a hotel famed for its vast high-end art collection, which includes the Picasso that owner Steve Wynn put his elbow through (before eventually having it restored and selling it to another collector in 2013 for $155 million).

The point is that, in Vegas, you have to be very careful about who you try to intimidate with talk of money. At Wynn's other hotel, the Bellagio, it was rumoured that a fight broke out after a man tried to join a game of blackjack where a multimillionaire Texan oil tycoon was losing his shirt. The oil barren attempted to pay off the gentleman with a fist of cash so he could continue to play alone. 'Wow, you must be worth a lot of money,' said the newcomer. 'Sure,' said the Texan, 'over a hundred mill. Now get lost.' 'Wow,' came the reply. 'I'll tell you what,' said the man. 'I'll flip you for the whole $100 million.' That man turned out to be an Australian media tycoon worth nearly $2 billion.

THE STEVE WYNN STORY

Football opens many doors, and it isn't long before even the richest people want to talk about what Wayne Rooney is like on the pitch, what the life of a footballer is *really* like. Usually, the process is easy, but every now and again you meet a man who could wipe out the UK deficit with a single swipe of his American Express Black Card, and the power to shock and impress is severely diminished because, for the most part, these people have been going at life in a major way right up to their first heart murmur at the age of forty.

Just the other summer I met up with a friend of mine. He is a good guy, very serious, but then with a net worth of £250 million I suppose he has to be. However, as long as you stick to the motto of 'never ask a man worth more than £100 million how he made his first million' you'll sort of be OK. What I've also found is that the impact of my stories has a limited effect on an individual worth over a certain amount of money. The only way to impress them is to tell them something that Wayne Rooney or Carlos Tevez once said to you on the pitch, because that is the one thing I have that their money can't buy. On this occasion, though, my friend actually asked me a question about my work – not a very good one, or necessarily about the game, but it was a question about football, and that hasn't happened too often.

We sat down to discuss our business, and he looked at me across the table while I waited for the inevitable. 'So, at the end of the season, is there one place that all the footballers generally go to let their hair down?' I thought about it for a moment. I needed a very decent anecdote to get across the fact that there are a host of very good reasons why footballers prefer the Las Vegas strip for their end-of-season antics. The Steve Wynn story is reserved for special guests – and with good reason: he has a habit of suing people.

For those of you who haven't heard of Steve Wynn, he is an American billionaire who spent and made a fortune building hotels on the Vegas strip, including the Mirage, Treasure Island, the Bellagio, the Encore and, probably because he felt he deserved it, the Wynn. He is personally worth around $3 billion and is the 491st richest person on the planet.

Upstairs, in the hotel's penthouse, were six lads who felt very important and more than a little cocksure of themselves.

'We wanna speak to Steve Wynn. Wynny, is he there? We're spending a fortune here. Put Wynny on!'

At the other end of the line, the operator said, 'Just a moment, sir, I'll try to reach him for you.'

Pardon?

And then a man answered the phone: 'Hi, Steve Wynn speaking.'

'Erm … yeah, hi, Mr Wynn, we're staying in the penthouse and we were wondering if the hotel could do anything for us?'

'You're in the penthouse, huh? Guys, meet me in the lobby in fifteen minutes.'

After a quick Google to see what the man looked like, we took the lift down towards the reception and walked into the lobby half-cut, in shorts, T-shirts and flip-flops. Standing in the middle of the floor, dressed in an immaculate suit, was Steve Wynn.

'Guys, are you having a good time with us?' he asked. We nodded. 'That's great. Listen, I gotta say I love the balls on you guys. I'll tell you what I'm gonna do for you. Take the cabana at the back of the pool for the day, hang out and enjoy the hotel, guys,' he said. The next bit has become the stuff of legend, because what we heard him say was, 'It's all on the house.' What he actually said was, 'Anything you want, just ask the butler.'

The champagne may as well have come in a keg; the long-legged girls, who made out they were on a trip but most certainly worked the area, played us like a fiddle and ordered lobsters, steaks, and called in more girls by the hour as the afternoon went from thrifty to financial suicide. At some point in the proceedings a fella turned up and began carving an ice sculpture. Despite the fact that Steve Wynn is almost blind these days, he saw us coming all the way down the strip.

You can't kid a fucking kidder. Not in Vegas. The final bill was over $70,000; the cabana alone was $25,000 for the day.

When I finished telling the story to my friend he carried on looking at the road through the window of his Porsche Cayenne and said, 'That's a good one,' with all the usual enthusiasm. 'Now, do you want to hear my Steve Wynn story?'

I slumped back into the car seat and listened.

Years before Wynn had taught me a lesson, he was the

undisputed king of the Vegas strip – everybody wanted to meet him, and it was in his interests to network with the world's highest rollers.

During a trip to the US, my friend (who we'll call Derek) and his wife (who we'll call a vulture) had been introduced to Wynn via a mutual friend. They'd hit it off immediately and were given a guided tour of the hotels and art collections before Wynn mentioned that he was hosting dinner and drinks on his boat in a couple of days' time and would they like to come along. It was a fantastic invitation and Derek and his wife duly turned up two days later at the monster yacht, moored on the coast, to be greeted by the staff, who offered them a glass of champagne as they went on deck.

'To my horror,' said Derek, 'there was a huge table at the back of the boat, with sixteen place settings. It was a rather more intimate affair than I had envisaged and, worse, I was now trapped. We sailed out to sea, dropped anchor, and I was introduced to the rest of the party.'

For legal reasons, I can't say who was there – all the names that follow are false – but you can probably make an assured guess at a couple of them. The party included some of the richest people on the planet: hedge-fund managers, social network moguls, media tycoons and entrepreneurs.

'We were summoned to sit down and, as the starters were served, Steve stood up to make what I thought was going to be a toast,' said Derek. 'Instead, he said, "OK, now seeing as we're all getting to know one another, I think each of the guys should stand up, tell us his name, what he does for a living, and how much he's worth. We'll go to my right."'

'I couldn't believe it,' said Derek. 'I looked around the table and realised that I was going to be last. I started sweating immediately. The first guy stood up. "Hi, I'm Marty Trueman, and when I left Goldman Sachs [laughter broke out, but I didn't know why] I founded a hedge fund called "Sterling & Sterling". We now have $4.2 billion of assets under management and I'm personally worth around $750 million." There was applause and he sat down. The next guy stood up. "Hey, everybody, I'm Todd Hendricks. I founded a social media company to bring together people in the business arena. Most of you I know are on it [more laughter]. We plan to raise an IPO early next year which would value the business at around $40 billion, which would make me around $10 billion personally."

'On it went. The next guy stood up. "Hi, I'm Marc Kristinsson and I founded a company that allows you to talk over the internet for free. I sold it for nearly $5 billion and I've recently purchased it again. I'm worth around $1 billion and I appreciate that not many of you care about saving money on your long-distance calls."

'More laughter. Eventually, it came round to me. I was the poorest person on the boat and felt embarrassed by it, which was ridiculous. I took a big glug of champagne and, in doing so, I suddenly had a moment of clarity. I looked straight at Steve Wynn and said, "Hi, everybody. I'm Sebastian Gottlieb. I own a number of fashion brands but, perhaps more importantly than that, I'm the most content person on this boat." They never invited me back after that.'

The truth is, no matter who you are and what you've done, you're never too rich to be taught a lesson. I don't care how much champagne you can afford.

APPENDIX

The Guide to Modern Football Language

Banter: The way that footballers talk to each other, the words and phrases they use, has remained largely unchanged for thirty or forty years. There are some new additions, but the context is the same. You can still hear BBC pundit Mark Lawrenson use the word 'shock' at the end of a sentence when he's being sarcastic. In the changing room I might read something out of the paper such as, 'It says here that Player X has been caught with his trousers down,' and half a dozen people will reply, 'Shock.'

Big time (massive): A player who enjoys giving the impression to teammates, opponents or the media that he is wealthy and has lots of desirable material objects. He will do this by posting pictures on his Instagram account every time he buys the latest pair of Christian Louboutins, or anything that most people would never be able to afford. On the pitch he will 'cash off' other players he knows are not earning as much money as he is. It's actually become rife in the game, especially amongst the kids coming through into the first team. I heard one kid say to another on our team that he could come and watch him play for England Under-21s if he liked, but that he might prefer instead to clean his new Mercedes that he'd just purchased. Ten minutes later, after overhearing the whole thing, one of our experienced professionals lifted him clean off his feet with an awful tackle. Lesson learned for both kids.

Bomb scare: A person who is likely to do something extremely random, often to the detriment of themselves and embarrassment of others, at any given moment. For example, 'Did you see Nile Ranger got arrested last night? He's a total bomb scare, him.'

Bomb squad: The reserve side, where players who aren't good enough for the first team, or are unfancied by the manager, reside. E.g., 'Where's Ben Arfa?' 'He's training with the bomb squad.'

Hollywood: Refers to a player who is unable to play a simple pass and will always try the most outrageous and difficult thing any time they have the ball on the pitch. They may constantly shoot from 35 yards with their wrong foot, or play the furthest diagonal pass possible. Some players have even been branded with this nickname for the majority of their careers. Their approach to the game rarely works.

Jacks: Shouted by a player who wants the man with the ball being played into him to leave it or dummy the ball. When calls such as 'mine' and 'leave it' were banned, players needed a generic name to use so that everybody was on the same page. It was 'Jacks' that stuck.

Jason Puncheon: Refers to a player who has a particularly beautiful wife. Instead of saying, 'He's punching above his weight', we simply say, 'Jason Puncheon' and everybody knows what you're talking about.

Knockdowns: Refers to hanging around a player on a night out – a player who is particularly liked by the ladies – and trying to get in with the friends of the woman he is talking to. E.g., 'Mate, let me get on your knockdowns tonight.'

Ledge: A term of endearment used by teammates to address or describe one another during the good times. It is also used as a descriptive term relating to an event or an occasion. E.g., 'Did you see Ronaldo's goal last night?' 'Yeah. It was ledge!'

Speedboat, no driver: Refers to a player who has blistering pace but no clue where he is supposed to be running or when. Controversially, this phrase is typically used for young black players. There are lots of managers who do not trust black players with the disciplined side of the game and just tell them to run instead – I even had a manager who did not want to play black centre-halves because he was convinced they had tunnel vision and didn't read the game well enough. I can't disprove it one way or another, though it sounds ridiculous to me. However, I'm here to tell you that lots of managers feel this way and I've lost count of managers, coaches, academy coaches and players who describe young black players using this term. It's even been said to me on the pitch by an opposition player when we brought on a young black player in the second half.

Tekkers: No player I've ever heard in training, or a match for that matter, in any team that I've ever played for, uses the word 'tekkers'. Just so you know. It's a word made up by TV people who want to give the impression that they're on the inside.

Third man run: Up, back and through. The third man run is a ball played up to the front man who then drops it off to a midfielder, who in turn plays the ball longer for another player, a third man, to run on to. It is most common in this guise but it works in most areas of the pitch.

Where's Beadle?: Refers to deceased television personality Jeremy Beadle, and is usually shouted from the back of a group of players who feel they are doing too much running, or are working too hard, and must be the subject of a hidden camera to see how much they can take.

Worldy: Reserved for a top-class goal or save. Also applies to girls.

ACKNOWLEDGEMENTS

Deloitte

Twitter

Forbes

Bloomberg Business Week

Danny Higginbotham

The suit at Nike – proof that no director of a sportswear
company should ever wear a suit

Jamie Oliver

The Secret Physio

The Secret Psychologist

INDEX